Frances Turnbull

Published by Musicaliti® Publishers
575 Tonge Moor Road, Bolton, BL2 3BN

Copyright © 2016 Musicaliti
ISBN 978-1-907935-69-5

All rights reserved. No part of this publication may be reproduced, stored in a retrieval system, or transmitted by any means, mechanical, photocopying, recording or otherwise, without the prior permission of the copyright holder.

Guitar Basics	5
Green Songs	9
Pink Songs	28
Yellow Songs	49
Blue Songs	71
Orange Songs	82
G Scale	104
Index	105

Guitar Basics

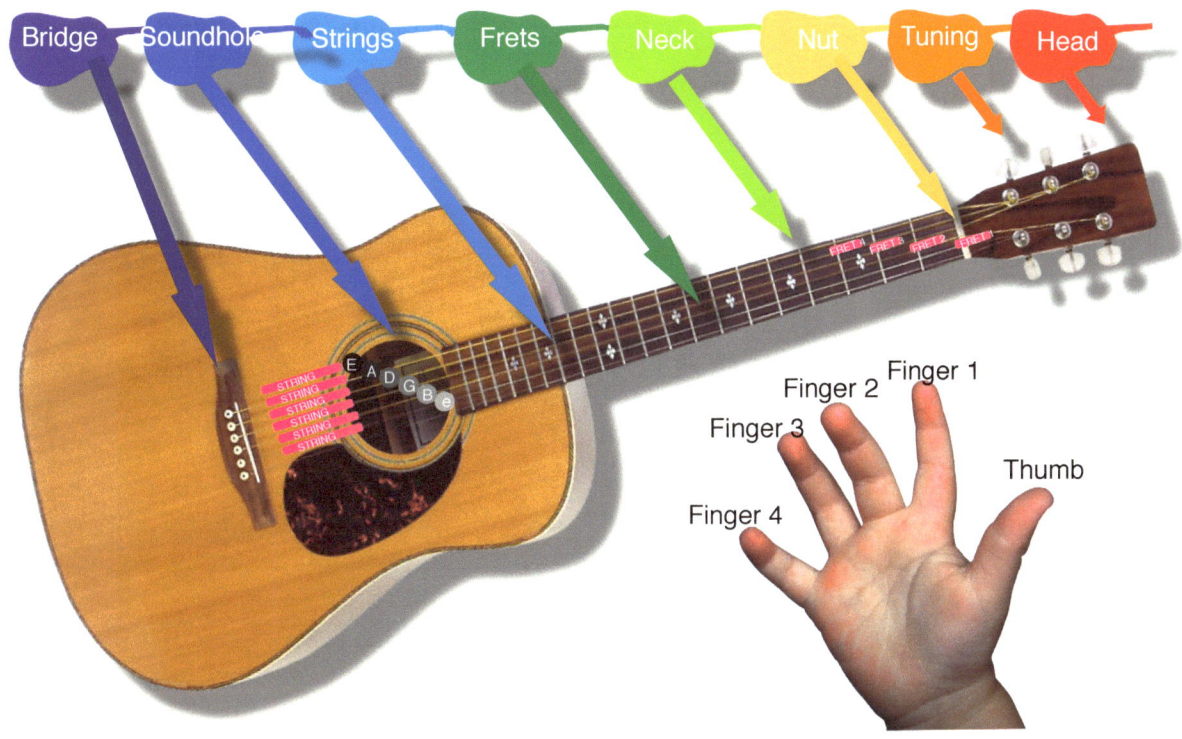

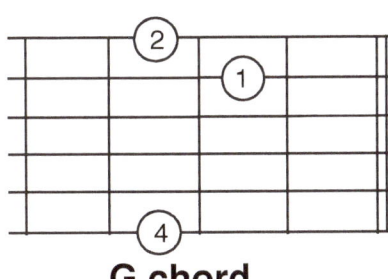

G chord

Guitar can be used to play tunes or **melodies** (one or a few notes at a time) or to accompany songs being sung - by playing all the strings with your fingers in the shape of a chord. The songs in this book are all in the chord of G. This means that you can play the G chord and sing along to the songs, or play the tune - it is a great skill to be able to do both! You could even have a guitar friend play the chord while you play the melody (tune) or the other way around! These pictures show the chords that we have used in this book. The numbers in circles show which finger to use!

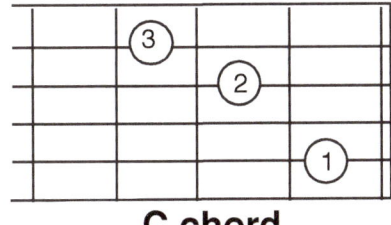

C chord

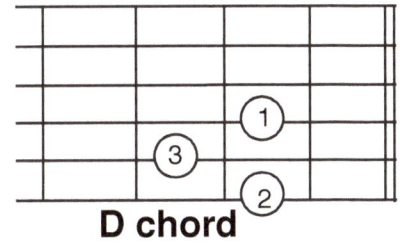

D chord

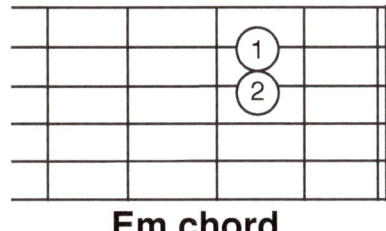

Em chord

How the notes work

The songs in this book are written in the **G scale**. **Green Songs** have the fewest notes as you get used to playing the notes of songs on the guitar, with more notes in **Pink Song**, **Yellow Songs**, **Blue Songs** and **Orange Songs**.

The notes in a G scale are: **G, A, B, C, D, E, F#**. On a **piano**, they look like this:

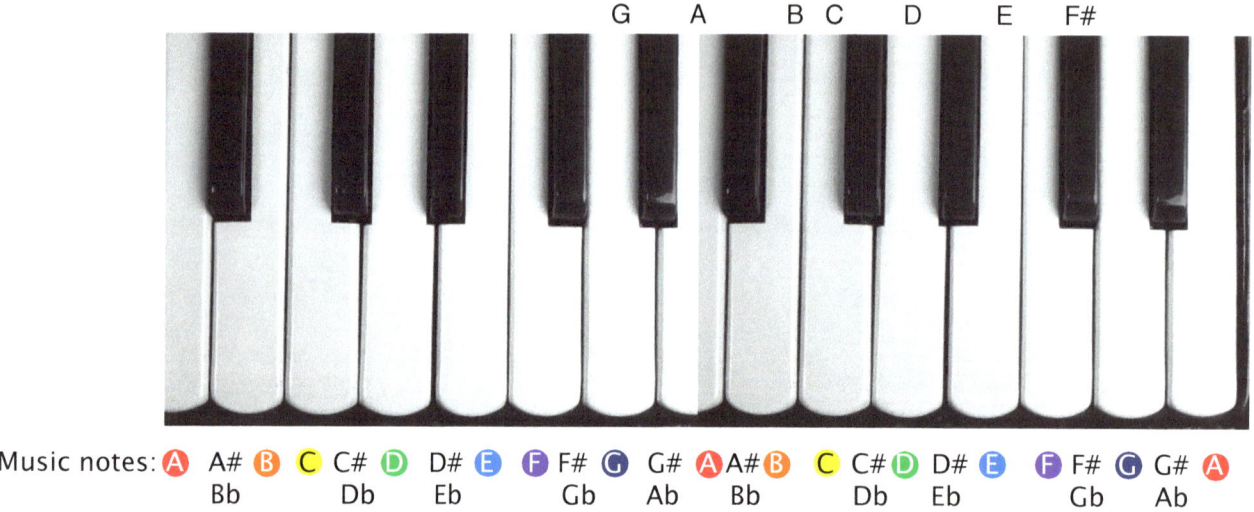

On a **guitar**, they look like this:
(guitar strings start with different notes/letters, and this picture shows the notes on the E string)

Scales have set gaps in between the notes, and the gaps between these notes determine when the black notes, or sharps and flats (also called accidentals) are used. Accidentals can be sharp (#) or flat (b), depending on the scale.

How the beats work

It's easy to focus on only playing the right notes, but we need to get the **long and short** beats right, too. It can be tricky to work out until we know what the lines and holes in the notes mean, so we can use **movement words** to remember how the beats sound. That way, you could say the movement words instead of the song words to remember how long to play the note!

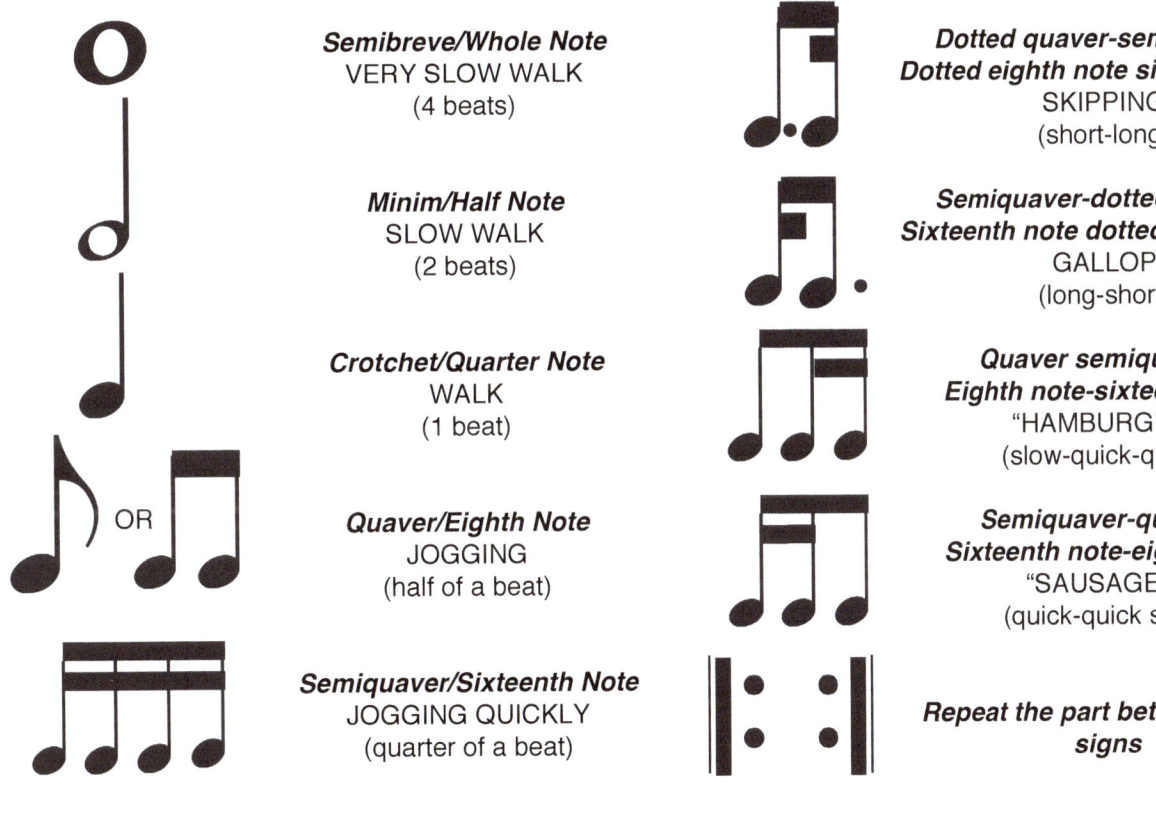

For example, if we sang the movement rhythms to "This Old Man", we would have:

Give it a try before singing the songs!

These pages introduce songs with 2 and 3 notes, and the different lengths of beats used:

E is on the 1st open string
D is on the 2nd string, 3rd fret
B is on the 2nd open string

1st string
2nd string
3rd string
4th string
5th string
6th string

Semibreve/Whole Note
VERY SLOW WALK
(4 beats)

Minim/Half Note
SLOW WALK
(2 beats)

Crotchet/Quarter Note
WALK
(1 beat)

 OR

Quaver/Eighth Note
JOGGING
(half of a beat)

Semiquaver/Sixteenth Note
JOGGING QUICKLY
(quarter of a beat)

*Dotted quaver-semiquaver /
Dotted eighth note sixteenth note*
SKIPPING
(short-long)

*Semiquaver-dotted quaver /
Sixteenth note dotted eighth note*
GALLOP
(long-short)

*Quaver semiquaver /
Eighth note-sixteenth note*
"HAMBURGER"
(slow-quick-quick)

*Semiquaver-quaver /
Sixteenth note-eighth note*
"SAUSAGES"
(quick-quick slow)

Repeat the part between these signs

Guitar Standard Tuning
E-A-D-G-B-E
♩ = 120

Traditional

Cobbler cobbler, mend my shoe, get it done by half past two,

Half past two is much too late, get it done by half past eight!

Next verse:

**Stitch it up and stitch it down
And I'll give you a half a crown**

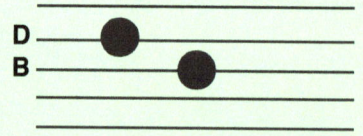

10

Traditional

Guitar Standard Tuning
E-A-D-G-B-E
♩= 120

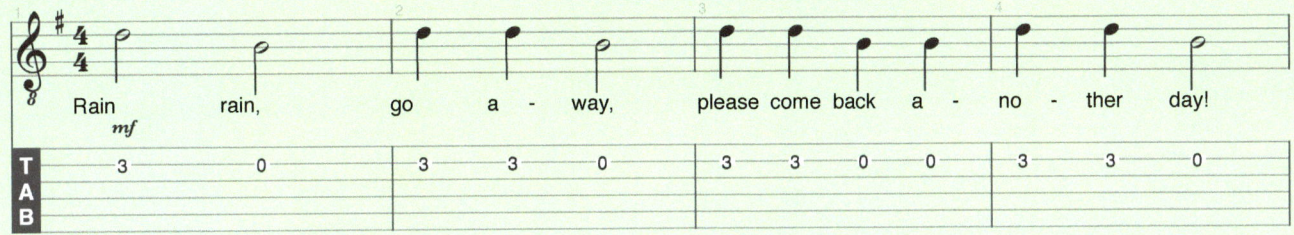

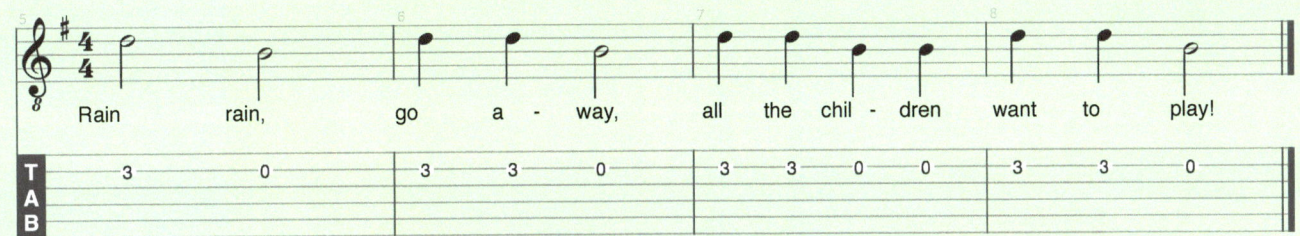

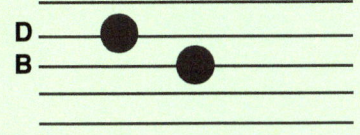

  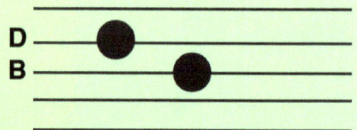

Guitar Standard Tuning
E-A-D-G-B-E
♩ = 120

Traditional

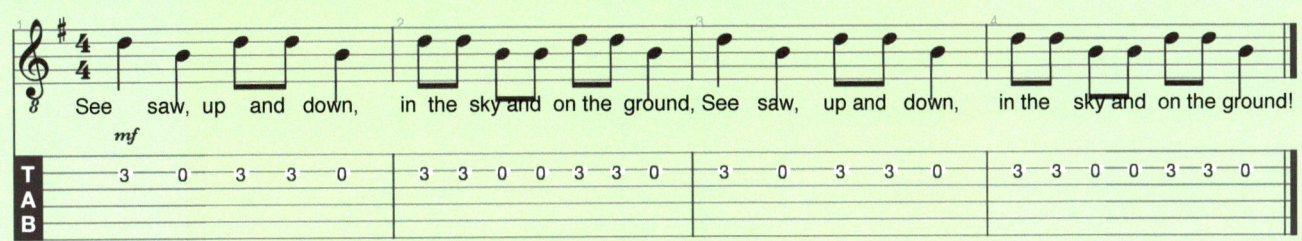

See saw, up and down, in the sky and on the ground, See saw, up and down, in the sky and on the ground!

Round and Round

Guitar Standard Tuning
E-A-D-G-B-E
♩ = 120

Traditional

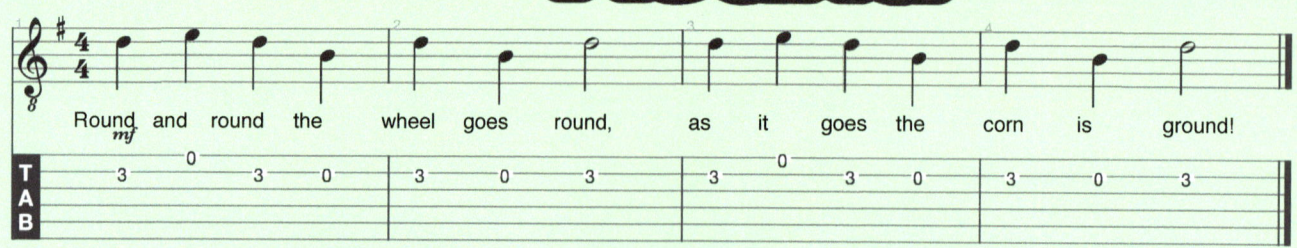

Round and round the wheel goes round, as it goes the corn is ground!

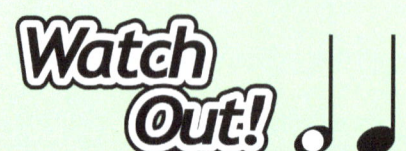

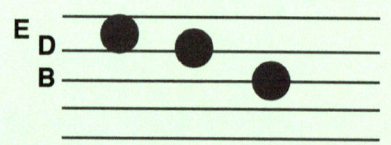

Guitar Standard Tuning
E-A-D-G-B-E
♩ = 120

Traditional

Lu - cy Loc - ket lost her poc - ket, Kit - ty Fi - sher found it,

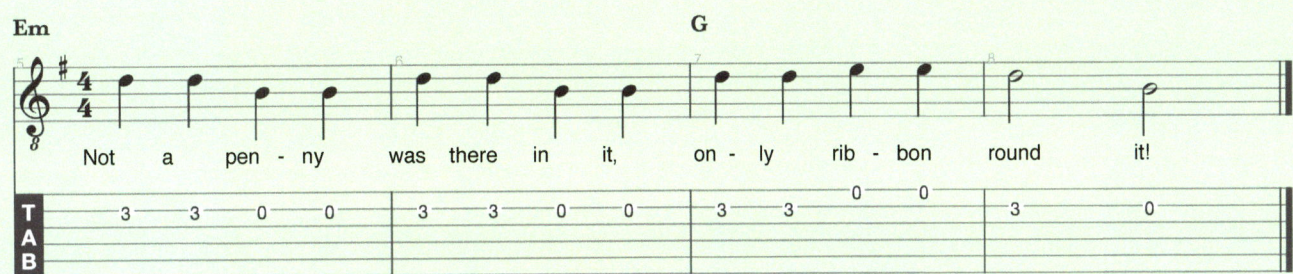

Not a pen - ny was there in it, on - ly rib - bon round it!

Guitar Standard Tuning
E-A-D-G-B-E
♩ = 120

Traditional

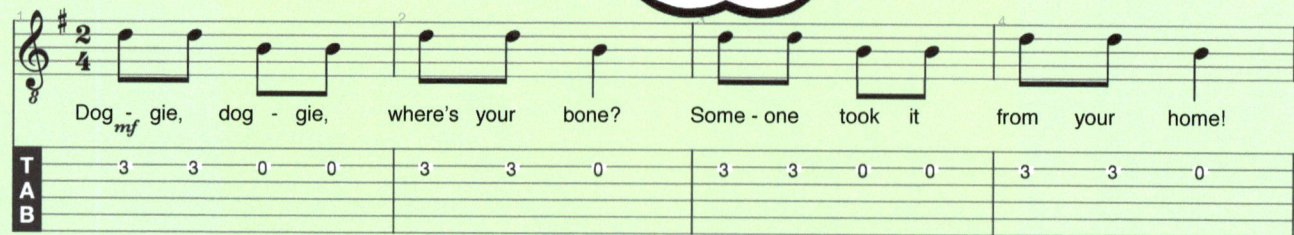

Dog - gie, dog - gie, where's your bone? Some - one took it from your home!

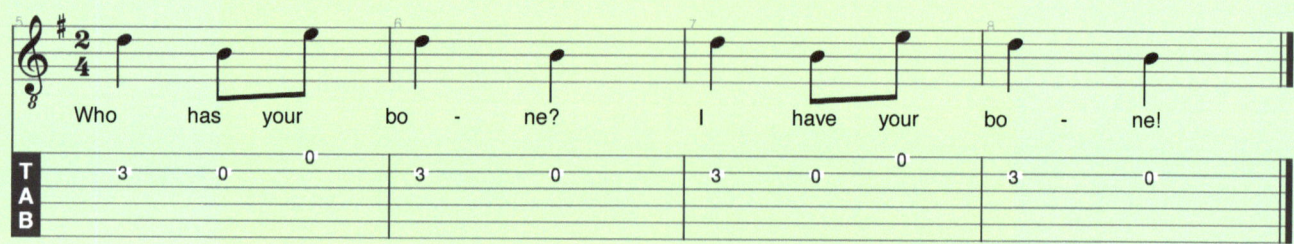

Who has your bo - ne? I have your bo - ne!

Snail Snail

Traditional

Guitar Standard Tuning
E-A-D-G-B-E
♩ = 120

G

Snail snail, snail, snail, creep a-round and round and round!

  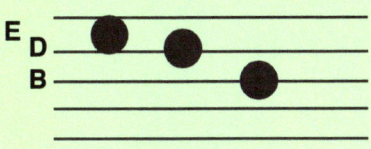

17

Guitar Standard Tuning
E-A-D-G-B-E
♩ = 120

Traditional

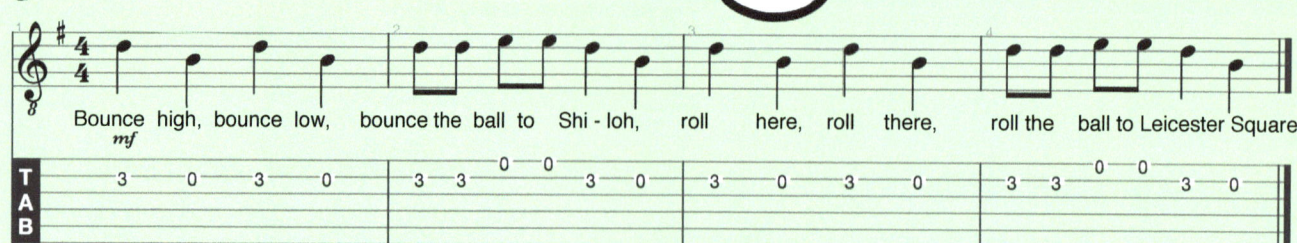

Bounce high, bounce low, bounce the ball to Shi-loh, roll here, roll there, roll the ball to Leicester Square

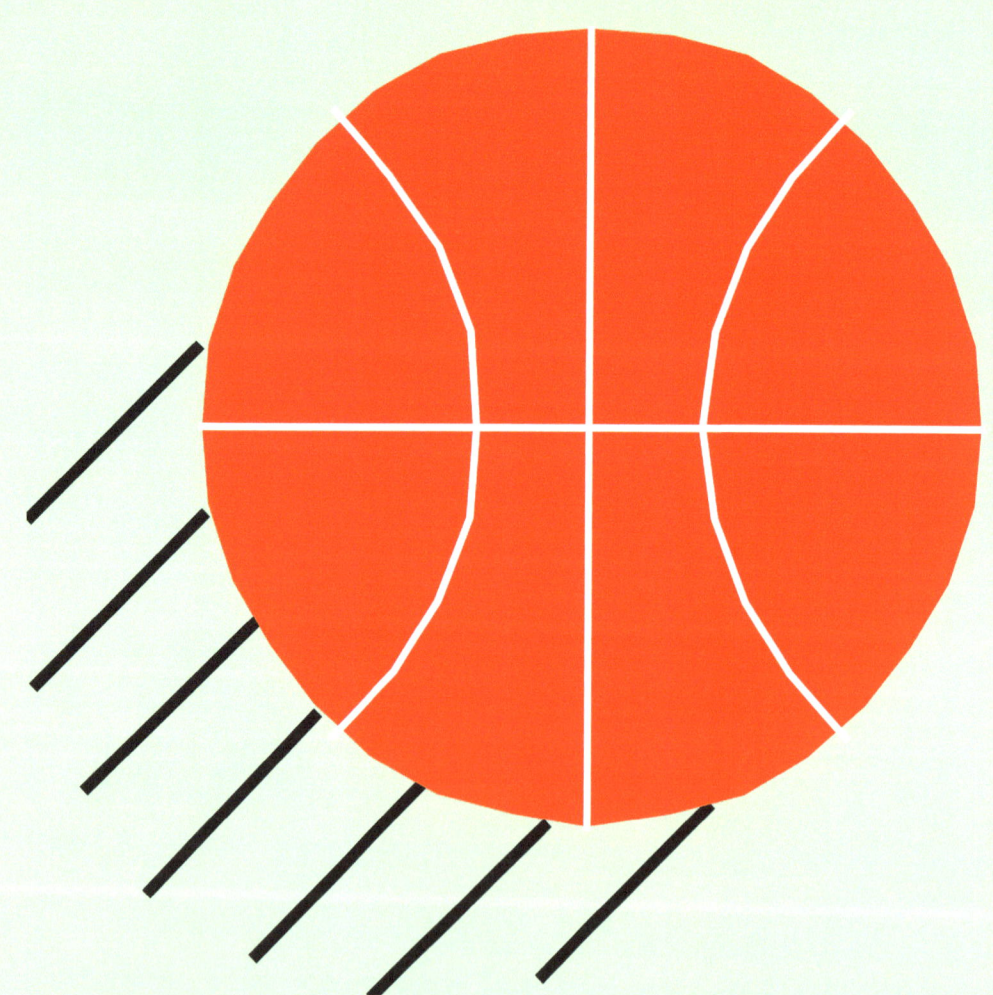

  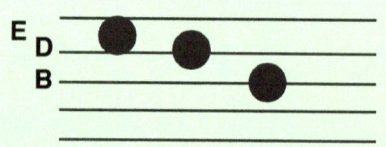

Guitar Standard Tuning
E-A-D-G-B-E
♩ = 120

Traditional

We are dan - cing in the fo - rest while the wolf is far a - way,

Who knows what may hap - pen to us if he finds us at our play!

Next verse:

**Wolf, are you there?
I'm combing my hair!
Wolf, are you there?
I'm coming to get you!**

  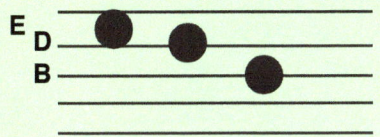

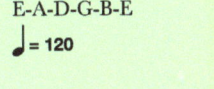

Guitar Standard Tuning
E-A-D-G-B-E
♩ = 120

Traditional

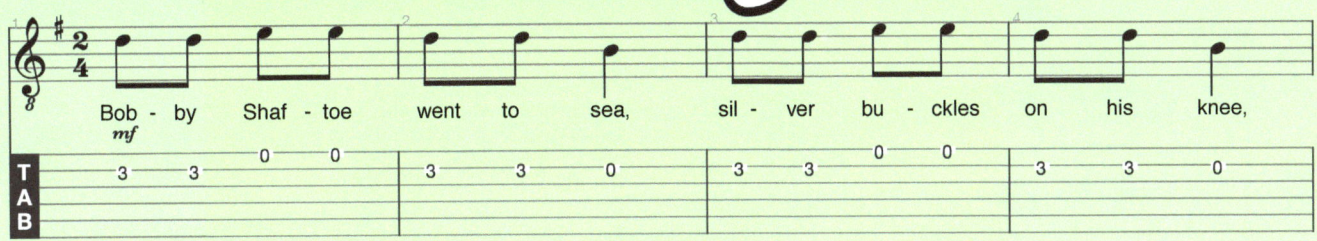

Bob - by Shaf - toe went to sea, sil - ver bu - ckles on his knee,

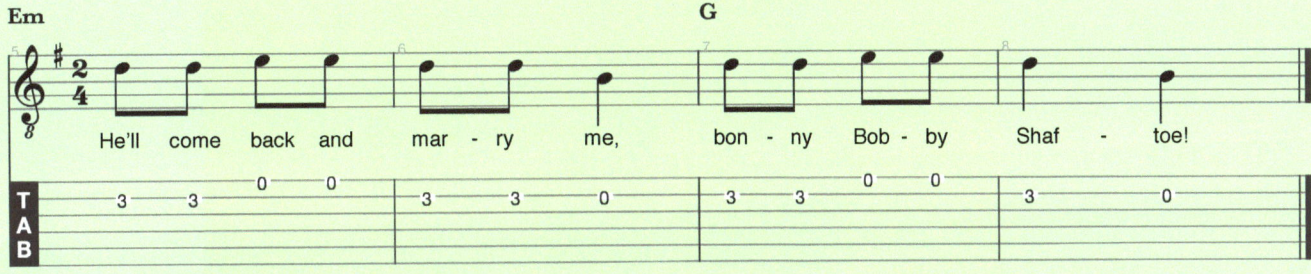

He'll come back and mar - ry me, bon - ny Bob - by Shaf - toe!

Next verse:

Bobby Shaftoe's fit and fair
Combing out his yellow hair
He's my love forevermore
Bonny Bobby Shaftoe

Bobby Shaftoe's looking out
All his ribbons flew about
All the ladies gave a shout,
Hey for Bobby Shaftoe

I had a Dog

Guitar Standard Tuning
E-A-D-G-B-E
♩ = 120

Traditional

I had a dog, his name is Ro-ver, e-very time I called his name, he rolled over and o-ver!

Next verse:

**Roll over, Rover
Roll over, Rover
Roll over, Rover
Pass him on!**

  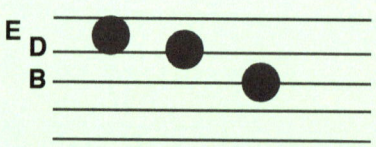

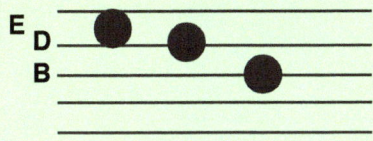

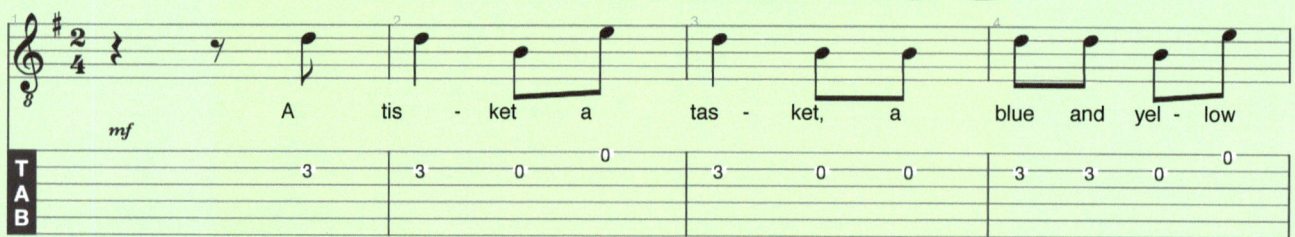
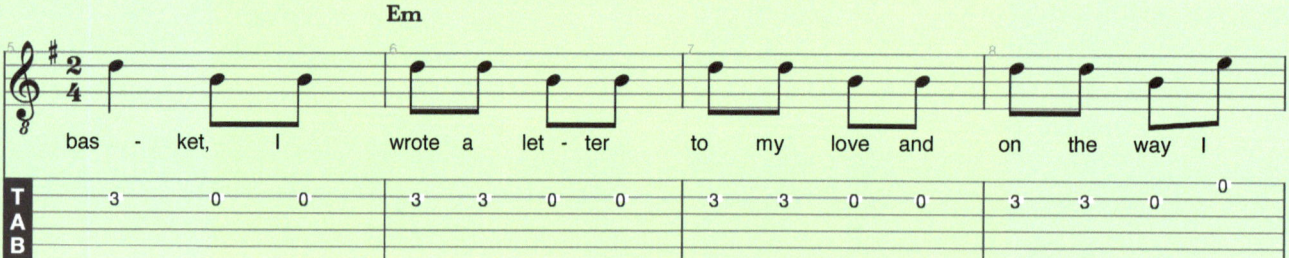
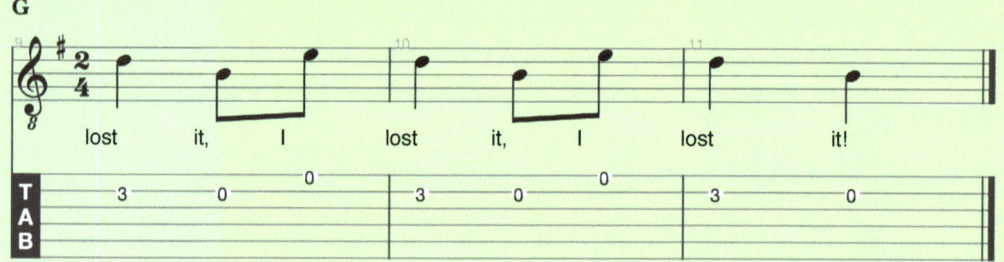

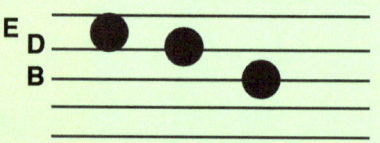

Guitar Standard Tuning
E-A-D-G-B-E
♩ = 120

Traditional

Lemonade Lemonade

Guitar Standard Tuning
E-A-D-G-B-E
♩ = 120

Traditional

G

Here we come! Where from? Bol - ton! What's your trade? Cot-ton mills and le-mon-ade! Give us some if you're not a - fraid!

  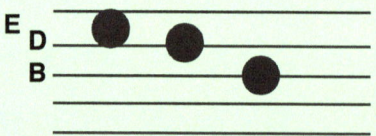

26

Guitar Standard Tuning
E-A-D-G-B-E
♩ = 120

Where are you going?

Traditional

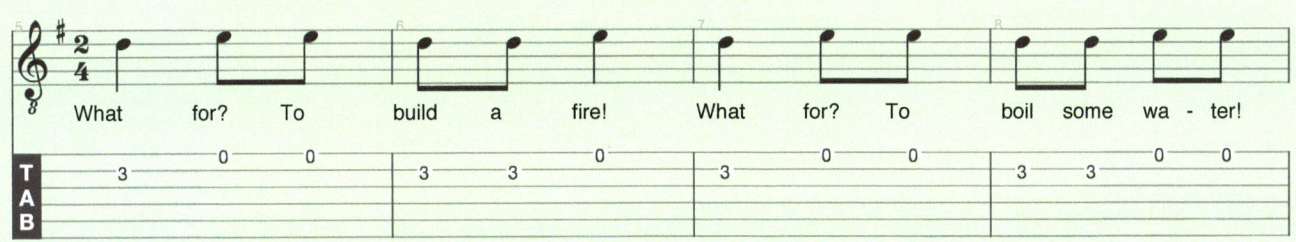

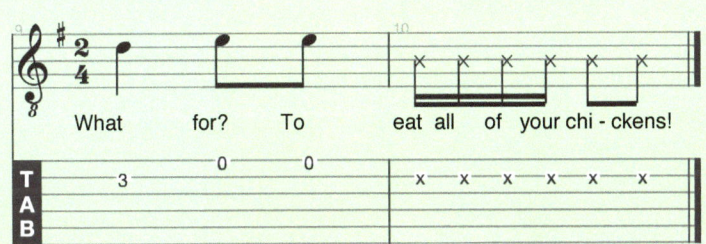

Watch Out!

27

These pages introduce songs with 3 and 4 notes, and the different lengths of beats used:

D is on the 2nd string, 3rd fret
C is on the 2nd string, 1st fret
B is on the 2nd open string
A is on the 3rd string, 2nd fret
G is on the 3rd open string
F# is on the 4th string, 4th fret
D is on the 4th open string

1st string
2nd string
3rd string
4th string
5th string
6th string

Semibreve/Whole Note
VERY SLOW WALK
(4 beats)

Minim/Half Note
SLOW WALK
(2 beats)

Crotchet/Quarter Note
WALK
(1 beat)

Quaver/Eighth Note
JOGGING
(half of a beat)

Semiquaver/Sixteenth Note
JOGGING QUICKLY
(quarter of a beat)

Dotted quaver-semiquaver / Dotted eighth note sixteenth note
SKIPPING
(short-long)

Semiquaver-dotted quaver / Sixteenth note dotted eighth note
GALLOP
(long-short)

Quaver semiquaver / Eighth note-sixteenth note
"HAMBURGER"
(slow-quick-quick)

Semiquaver-quaver / Sixteenth note-eighth note
"SAUSAGES"
(quick-quick slow)

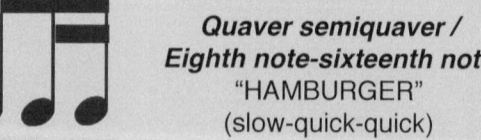

Repeat the part between these signs

28

Hickory Dickory

Guitar Standard Tuning
E-A-D-G-B-E
♩ = 120

Traditional

Hi - cko - ry Di - cko - ry but - ter - cup, how ma - ny fin - gers do I hold up?

Four you see and four you say, will you count four with me to - day?

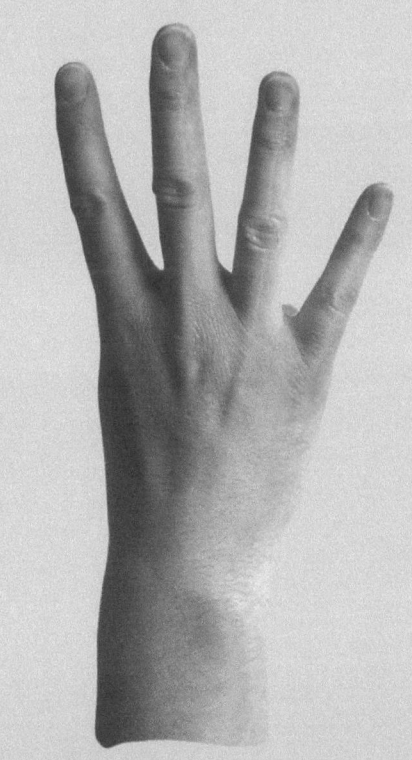

Guitar Standard Tuning
E-A-D-G-B-E
♩ = 120

Traditional

Pease por-ridge hot, pease por-ridge cold, pease por-ridge in the pot, nine days old,

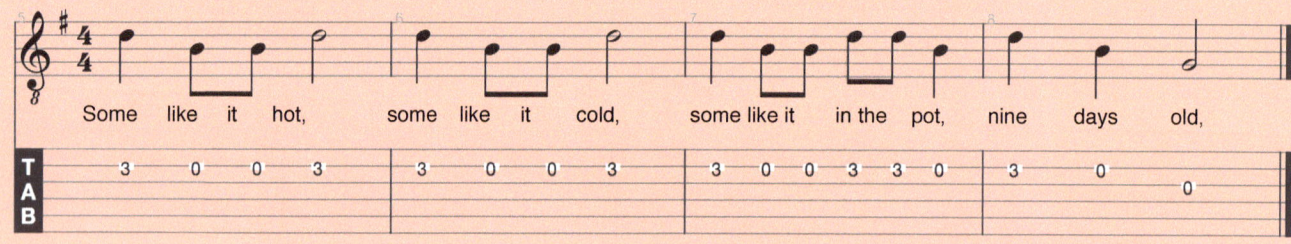

Some like it hot, some like it cold, some like it in the pot, nine days old,

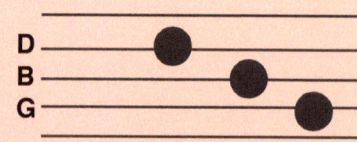

Guitar Standard Tuning
E-A-D-G-B-E
♩ = 120

Traditional

An-dy Pan-dy, su-gar and can-dy, all jump up!

Next verse:

Andy Pandy, sugar and candy
All jump down
Andy Pandy, sugar and candy
All jump in
Andy Pandy, sugar and candy
All jump out!

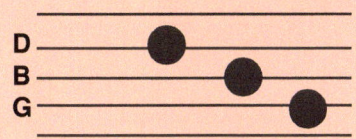

Guitar Standard Tuning
E-A-D-G-B-E
♩ = 120

Traditional

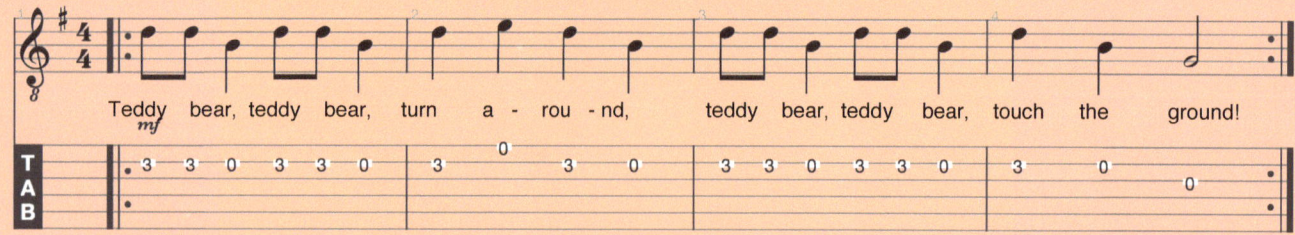

Teddy bear, teddy bear, turn a-round, teddy bear, teddy bear, touch the ground!

Next verses:

Teddy bear, teddy bear
Tie your shoe
Teddy bear, teddy bear
I love you

Teddy bear, teddy bear
Climb the stairs
Teddy bear, teddy bear
Say your prayers
Teddy bear, teddy bear
Turn off the light
Teddy bear, teddy bear
Say goodnight!

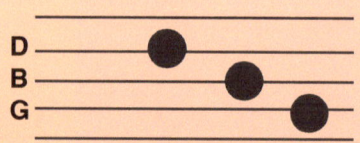

Guitar Standard Tuning
E-A-D-G-B-E
♩= 120

Traditional

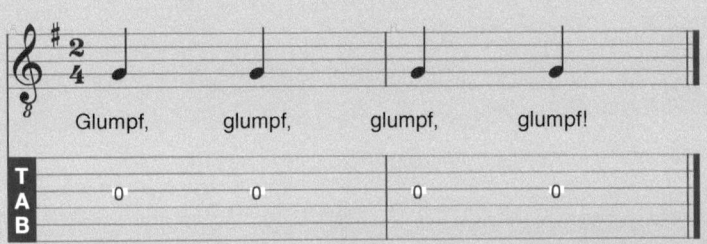

On a log, mis-ter frog, sang his song the whole day long,

Glumpf, glumpf, glumpf, glumpf!

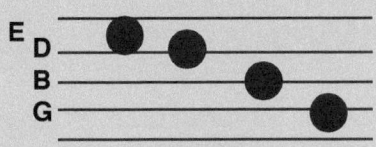

Apple Tree

Traditional

Guitar Standard Tuning
E-A-D-G-B-E
♩ = 120

G

Ap - ple tree, ap - ple tree, will your ap - ple fall on me,

I won't cry and I won't shout, if your ap - ple knocks me out!

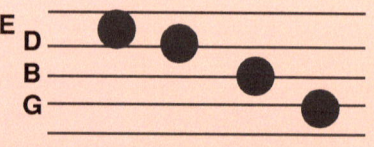

Guitar Standard Tuning
E-A-D-G-B-E
♩ = 120

Traditional

Let us chase the squir-rel, up the hick'ry, down the hick'ry, let us chase the squir-rel, up the hick'ry tree!

mf

Tab:
0 0 2 2 0 3 | 0 0 2 2 0 0 2 2 | 0 0 2 2 0 3 | 0 0 2 2 0

Guitar Standard Tuning
E-A-D-G-B-E
♩ = 120

Traditional

Ickle ockle, blue bottle, fishes in the sea, if you want a part-ner, just choose me!

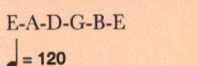

Guitar Standard Tuning
E-A-D-G-B-E
♩ = 120

Traditional

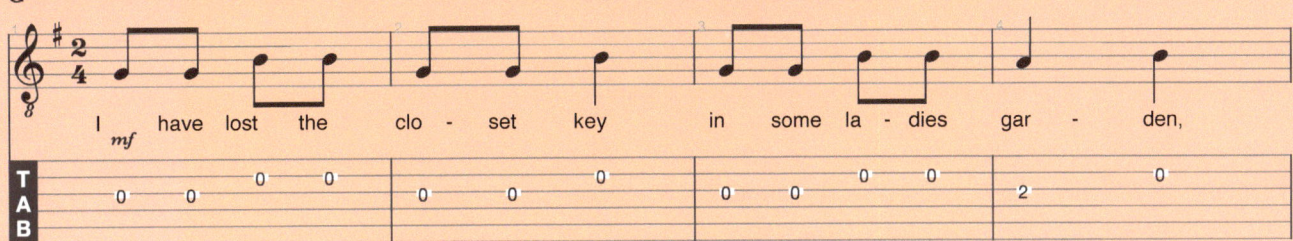

I have lost the clo-set key in some la-dies gar-den,

Help me find my clo-set key, in some la-dies gar-den!

  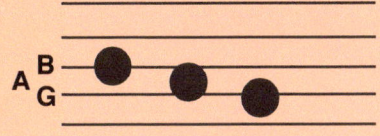

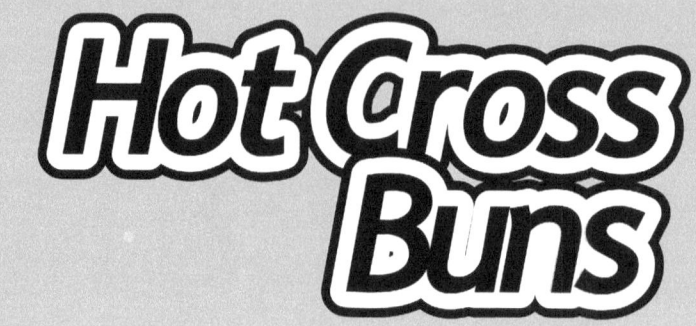

Hot Cross Buns

Guitar Standard Tuning
E-A-D-G-B-E
♩= 120

Traditional

Watch Out!

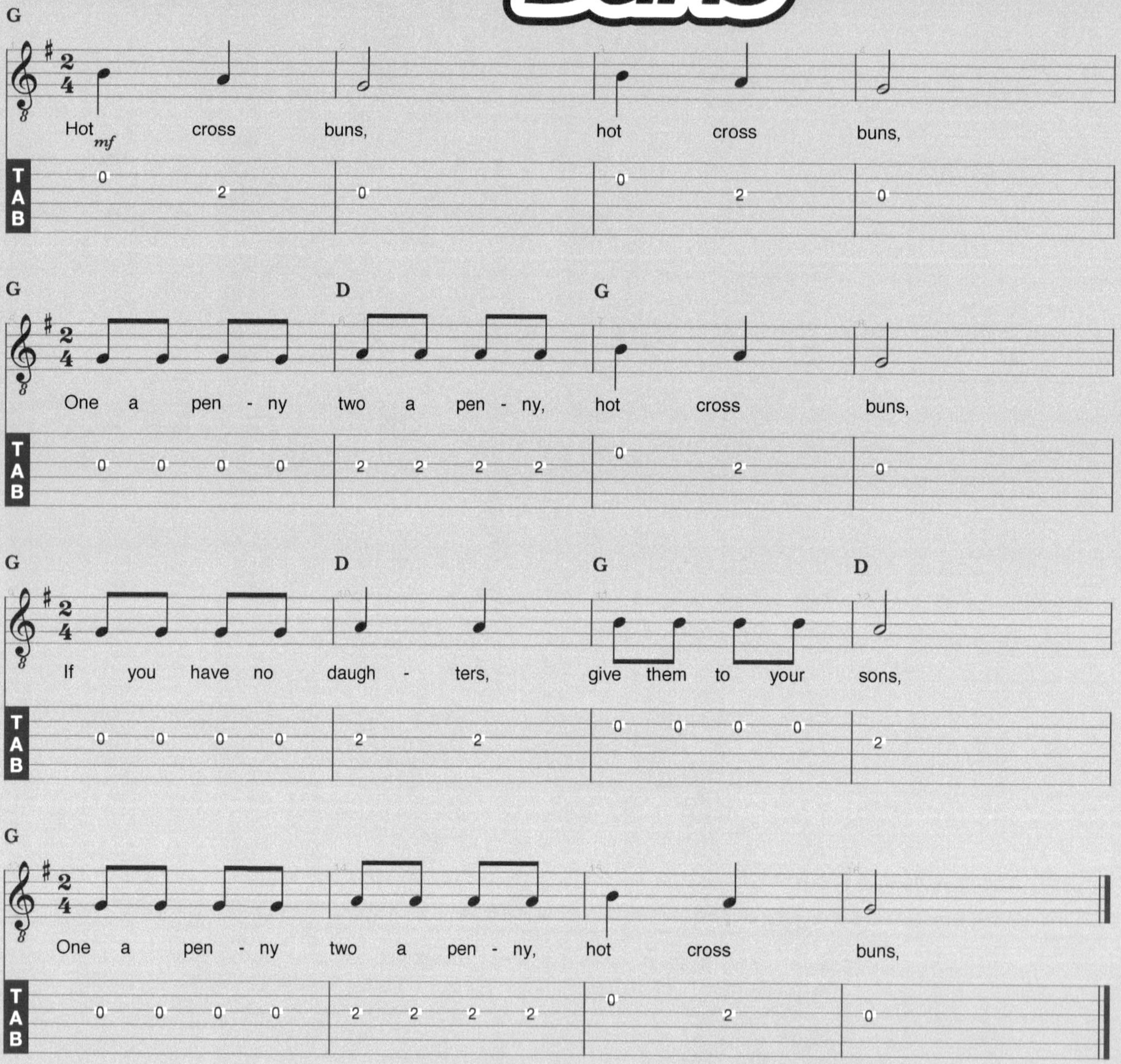

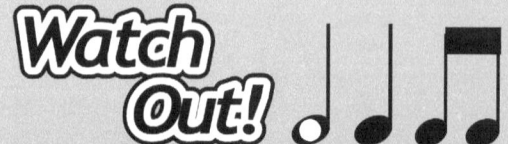

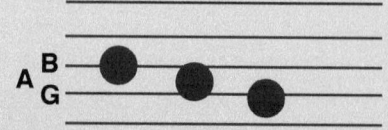

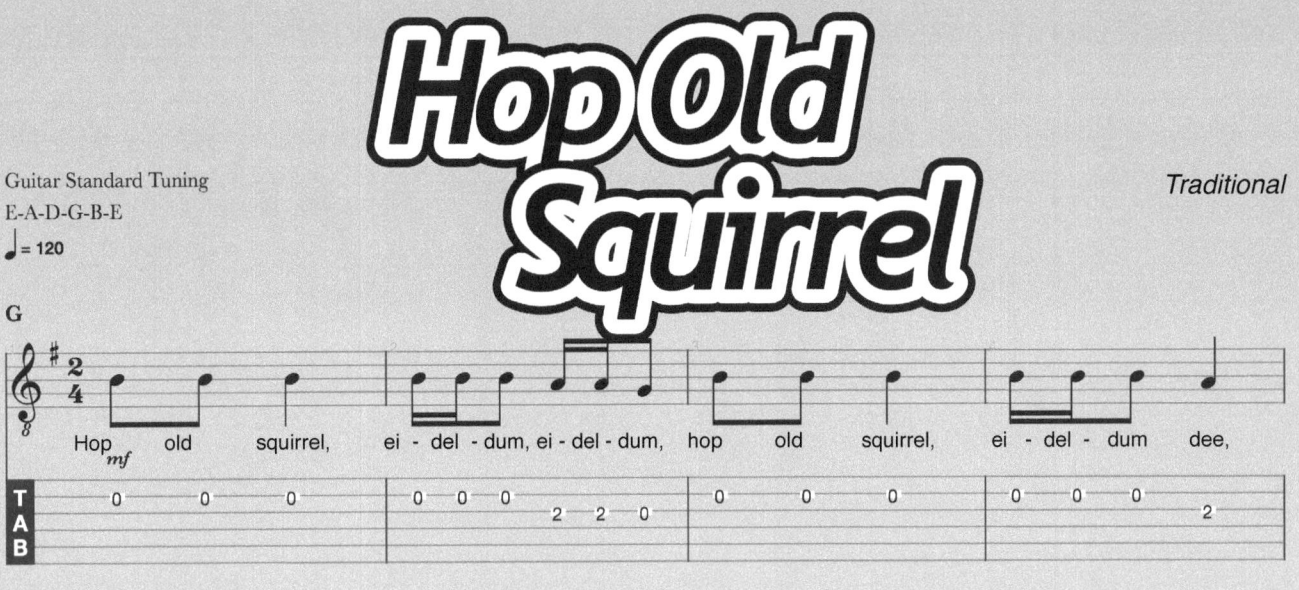

Mary had a Little Lamb

Traditional

Guitar Standard Tuning
E-A-D-G-B-E
♩ = 120

| G | | D | G |

Ma - ry had a lit - tle lamb, lit - tle lamb, lit - tle lamb,

| G | | D | G |

Ma - ry had a lit - tle lamb, it's fleece was white as snow!

Next verses:

He followed her to school one day
School one day, school one day
He followed her to school one day
Which was against the rules

It made the children laugh and play
Laugh and play, laugh and play
It made the children laugh and play
To see a lamb at school

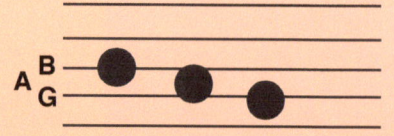

40

Riding in a Buggy

Guitar Standard Tuning
E-A-D-G-B-E
♩= 120

Traditional

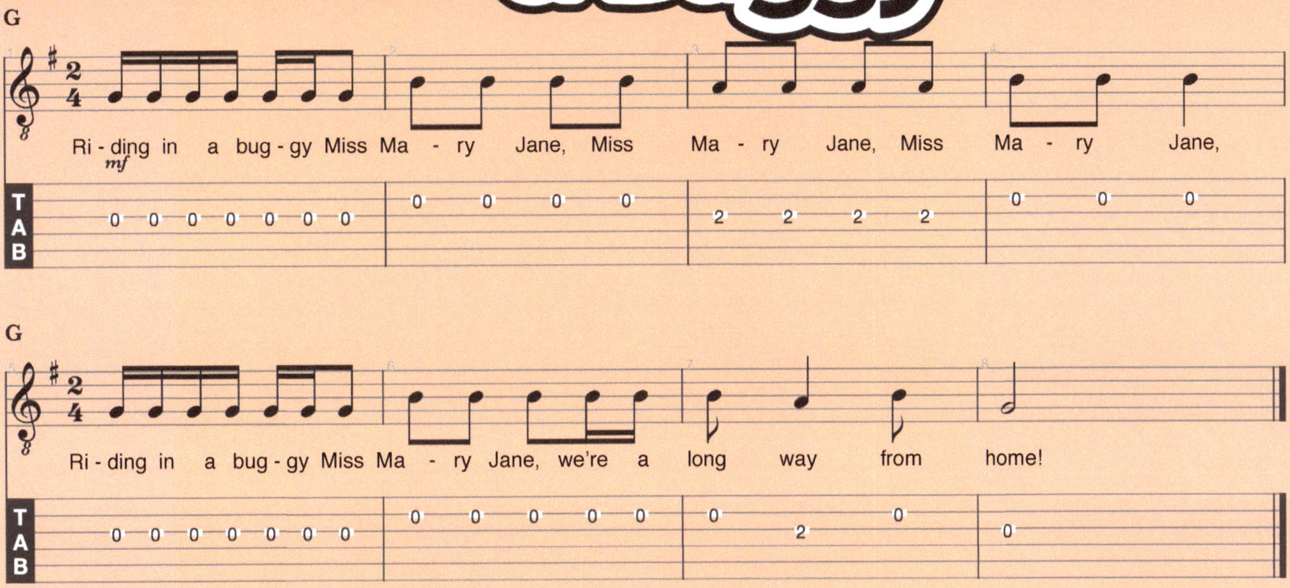
G
Ri - ding in a bug - gy Miss Ma - ry Jane, Miss Ma - ry Jane, Miss Ma - ry Jane,
mf
TAB
G
Ri - ding in a bug - gy Miss Ma - ry Jane, we're a long way from home!
TAB

Watch Out!
A
B
G

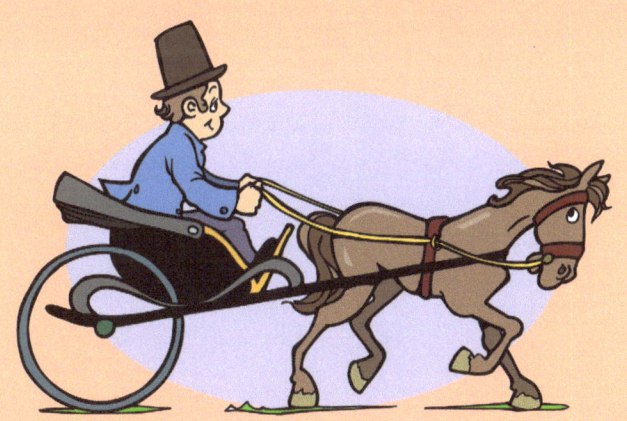

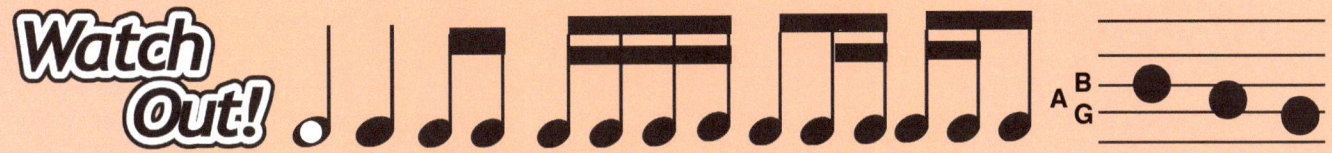

Guitar Standard Tuning
E-A-D-G-B-E
♩ = 120

Traditional

Ro - sie dar - ling, Ro - sie, ha ha Ro - sie

Ro - sie dar - ling, Ro - sie, ha ha Ro - sie

Way down, yon-der by Bal - ti - more, ha ha Ro - sie

Need no car - pet on the floor, ha ha Ro - sie

   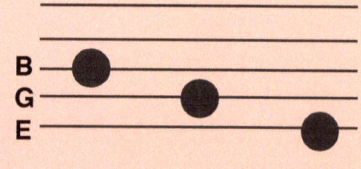

Go Round the Mountain

Guitar Standard Tuning
E-A-D-G-B-E
♩ = 120

Traditional

| G | | Em | G |

Go round the mountain, toa-die diddleum, toadie diddleum, go round the mountain, toadie diddleum dee!

mf

Next verses:

Tiptoe round the mountain
Toadie, diddle-um, toadie, diddle-um
Tiptoe round the mountain
Toadie, diddle-um, dee

Stomp round the mountain
Toadie, diddle-um, toadie, diddle-um
Stomp round the mountain
Toadie, diddle-um, dee

Skip round the mountain
Toadie, diddle-um, toadie, diddle-um
Skip round the mountain
Toadie, diddle-um, dee

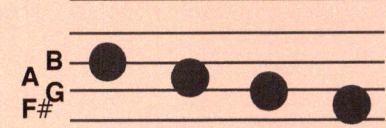

43

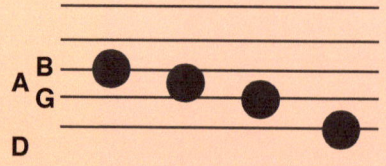

Come Butter Come

Guitar Standard Tuning
E-A-D-G-B-E
♩ = 120

Traditional

Come, but-ter, come, come, but-ter, come,

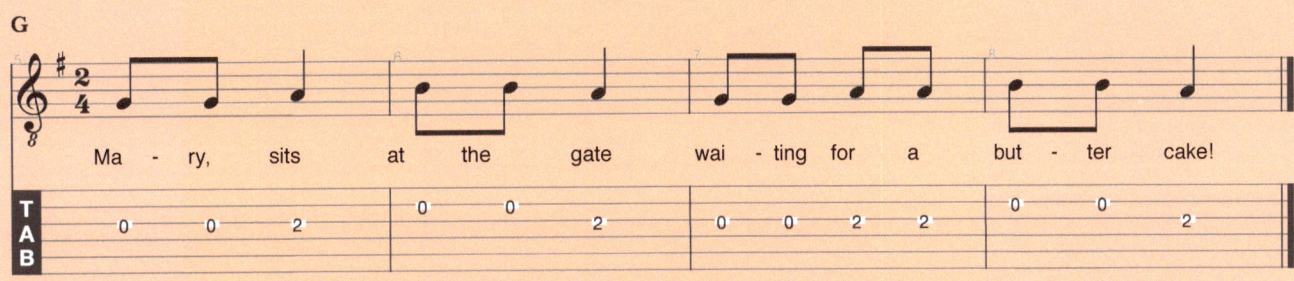

Ma-ry, sits at the gate wai-ting for a but-ter cake!

  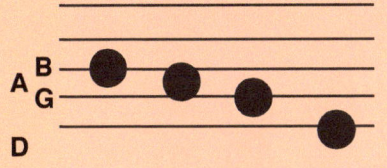

Old Mister Rabbit

Guitar Standard Tuning
E-A-D-G-B-E
♩ = 120

Traditional

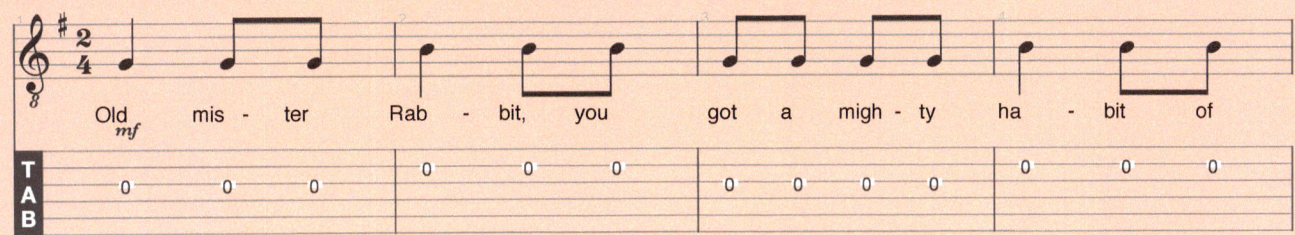

Old mis-ter Rab-bit, you got a migh-ty ha-bit of

Jum-ping in my gar-den and ea-ting all my cab-bage!

  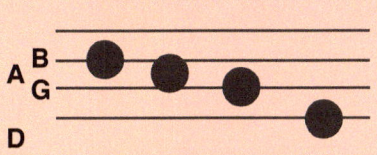

47

Hey Jim-a-Long

Guitar Standard Tuning
E-A-D-G-B-E
♩ = 120

Traditional

Hey Jim a-long, Jim a-long Jo-sie, Hey Jim a-long, Jim a-long Jo!

Watch Out!

Yellow Songs

These pages introduce songs with 5 notes, and the different lengths of beats used:

E is on the 1st open string
D is on the 2nd string, 3rd fret
B is on the 2nd open string
A is on the 3rd string, 2nd fret
G is on the 3rd open string
F# is on the 4th string, 4th fret
E is on the 4th string, 2nd fret

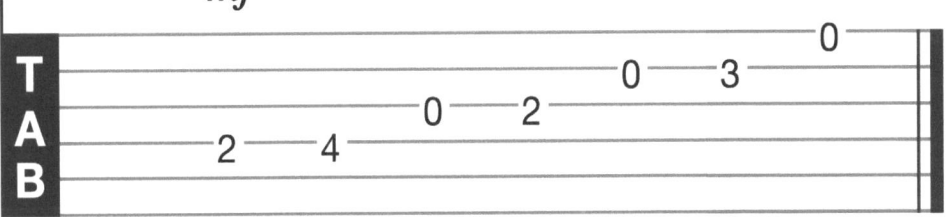

1st string
2nd string
3rd string
4th string
5th string
6th string

Semibreve/Whole Note
VERY SLOW WALK
(4 beats)

Minim/Half Note
SLOW WALK
(2 beats)

Crotchet/Quarter Note
WALK
(1 beat)

Quaver/Eighth Note
JOGGING
(half of a beat)

Semiquaver/Sixteenth Note
JOGGING QUICKLY
(quarter of a beat)

***Dotted quaver-semiquaver /
Dotted eighth note sixteenth note***
SKIPPING
(short-long)

***Semiquaver-dotted quaver /
Sixteenth note dotted eighth note***
GALLOP
(long-short)

***Quaver semiquaver /
Eighth note-sixteenth note***
"HAMBURGER"
(slow-quick-quick)

***Semiquaver-quaver /
Sixteenth note-eighth note***
"SAUSAGES"
(quick-quick slow)

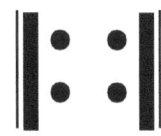

Repeat the part between these signs

49

Next verse:

And if that mocking bird don't sing
Mamma's gonna buy you a diamond ring
If that diamond ring turns brass
Mamma's gonna buy you a looking glass
And if that looking glass gets broke
Mamma's gonna buy you a billy goat
If that billy goat don't pull
Mamma's gonna buy you a cart and bull
If that cart and bull turn over
Mamma's gonna buy you a dog named Rover
If that dog named Rover don't bark
Mamma's gonna buy you a horse and cart
And if that horse and cart fall down
You'll still be the sweetest little baby in town!

Oats and Beans

Traditional

Guitar Standard Tuning
E-A-D-G-B-E
♩ = 120

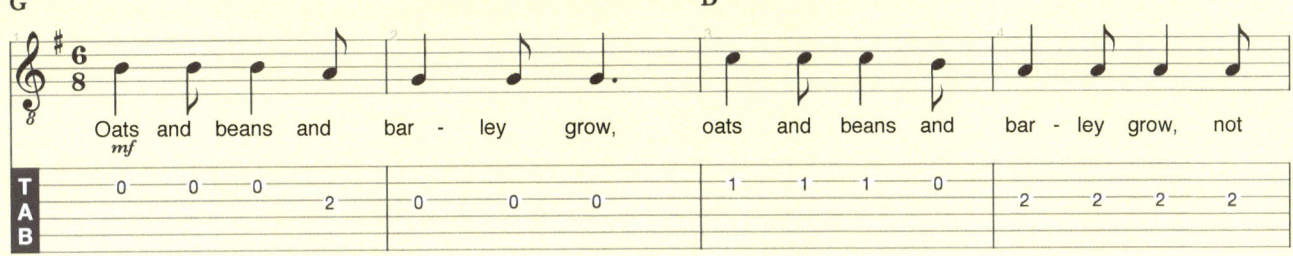

Oats and beans and bar-ley grow, oats and beans and bar-ley grow, not

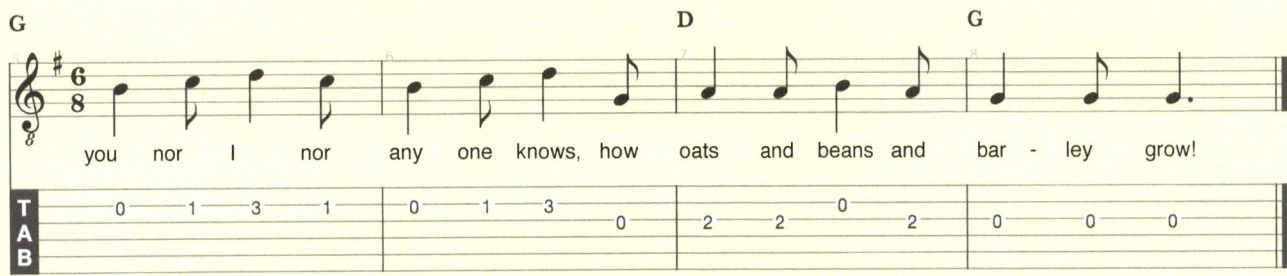

you nor I nor any one knows, how oats and beans and bar-ley grow!

Next verses:

First the farmer sows the seed
Stands up tall and takes his ease
Stamps his foot and claps his hands
And turns around to view the land

Waiting for a partner
Waiting for a partner
Not you nor I nor anyone knows I'm
Waiting for a partner

Dancing with a partner
Dancing with a partner
Both you and I and everyone knows I'm
Dancing with a partner

  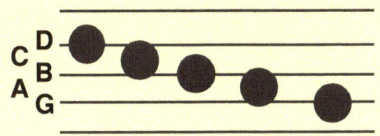

Guitar Standard Tuning
E-A-D-G-B-E
♩ = 120

Traditional

Once a man fell in a well, splish, splash, splosh it sounded, if he had not put it in, he would not have drown - ded!

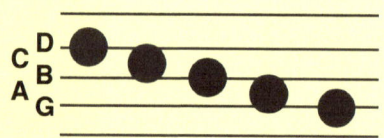

Guitar Standard Tuning
E-A-D-G-B-E
♩ = 120

Traditional

Fros-ty wea-ther, sno-wy, wea-ther,
when the wind blows, we all get to-ge-ther!

Sally go round the Sun

Guitar Standard Tuning
E-A-D-G-B-E
♩ = 120

Traditional

G   G

Sal - ly go round the sun,   Sal - ly go round the moon,

Sal - ly go round the chim - ney top   Sun - day af - ter - noon!

      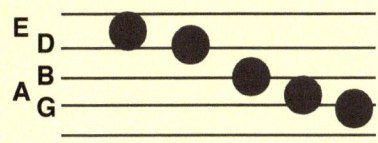

55

Around the Buttercup

Guitar Standard Tuning
E-A-D-G-B-E
♩ = 120

Traditional

All a-round the but-ter-cup, one, two, three,

If you want an awe-some friend, just choose me!

56

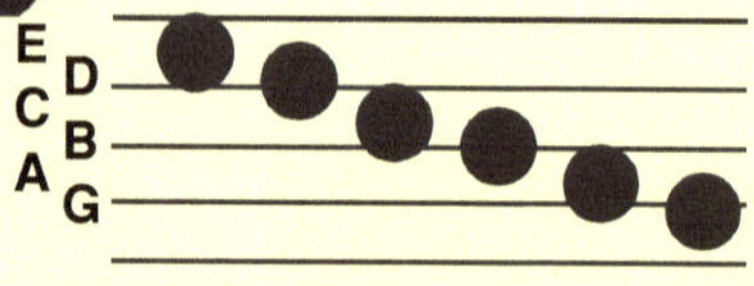

Who Did All the Baking?

Traditional

Guitar Standard Tuning
E-A-D-G-B-E
♩ = 120

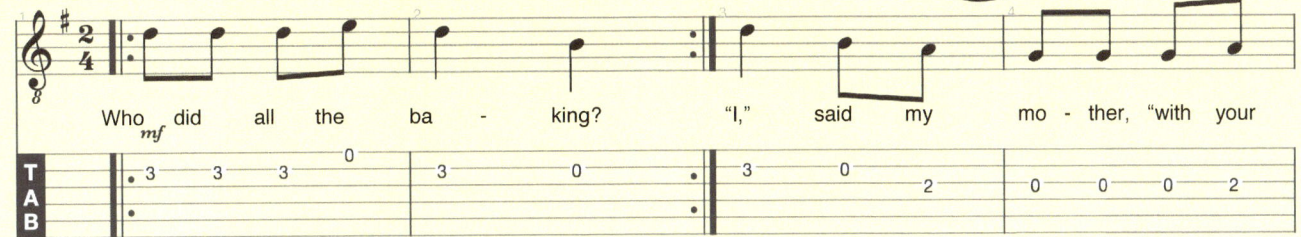

Who did all the ba-king? "I," said my mo-ther, "with your

lit-tle ba-by bro-ther, it was I, it was I!"

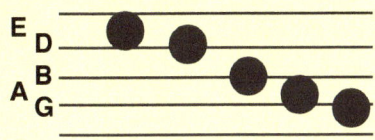

Here Comes a Bluebird

Guitar Standard Tuning
E-A-D-G-B-E
♩ = 120

Traditional

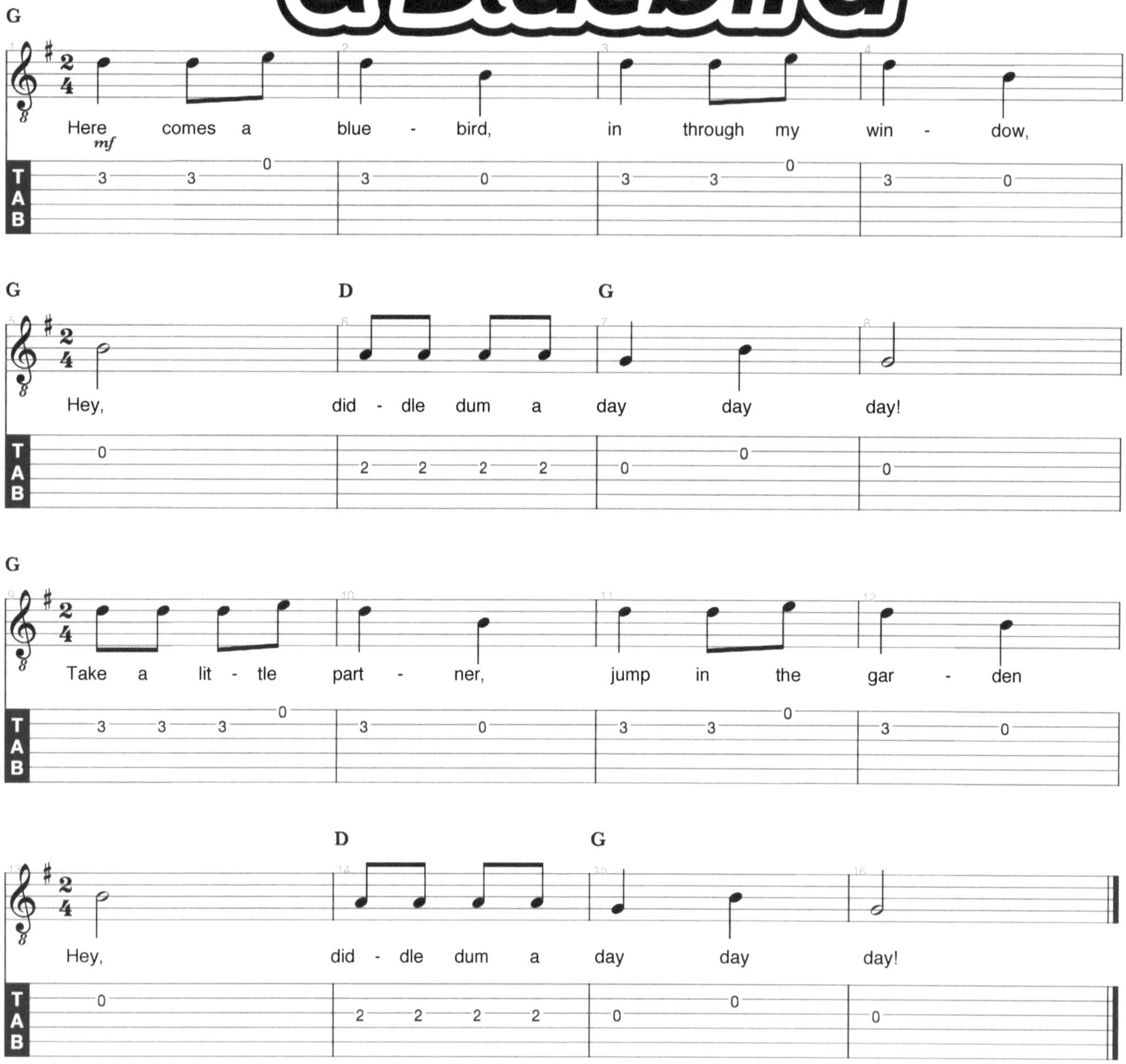
G
Here comes a blue - bird, in through my win - dow,
mf
G D G
Hey, did - dle dum a day day day!
G
Take a lit - tle part - ner, jump in the gar - den
D G
Hey, did - dle dum a day day day!
TAB

Watch Out!

E
D
B
A
G

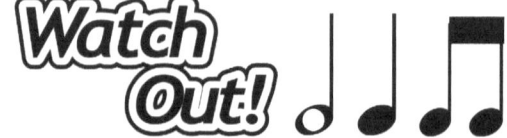

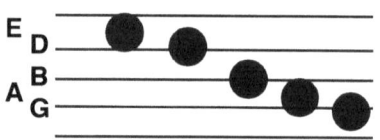

Johnny Works

Guitar Standard Tuning
E-A-D-G-B-E
♩ = 120

Traditional

John - ny works with one ham - mer, one ham - mer, one ham - mer,
John - ny works with one ham - mer, now he works with two!

Next verses:

Johnny works with two hammers
Two hammers, two hammers
Johnny works with two hammers
Now he works with three

Johnny works with three hammers
Two hammers, three hammers
Johnny works with three hammers
Now he works with four

Johnny works with four hammers
Two hammers, four hammers
Johnny works with four hammers
Now his work is done

Guitar Standard Tuning
E-A-D-G-B-E

♩ = 120

Traditional

Who's that knocking on my win-dow? who's that knocking on my door?

A - lly's knocking on my win - dow, A - lly's knocking on my door!

Bought me a Cat

Traditional

Guitar Standard Tuning
E-A-D-G-B-E
♩ = 120

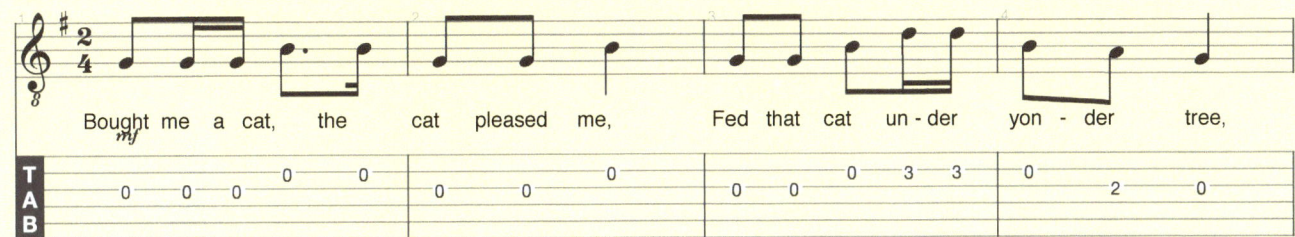

Bought me a cat, the cat pleased me, Fed that cat un-der yon-der tree,

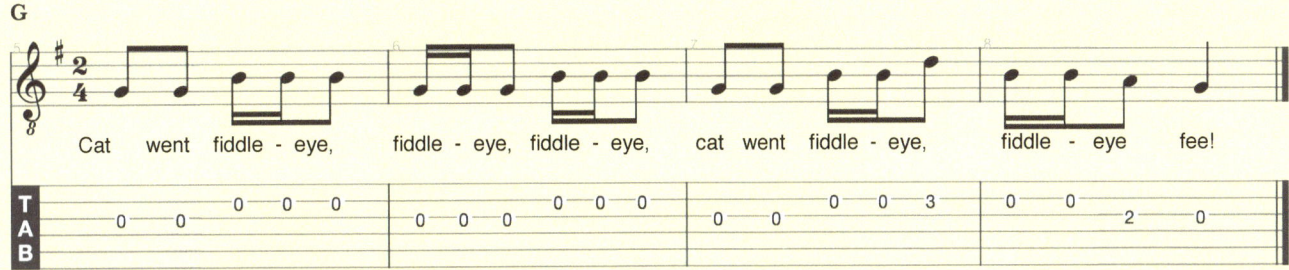

Cat went fiddle-eye, fiddle-eye, fiddle-eye, cat went fiddle-eye, fiddle-eye fee!

Next verses:

Bought me a hen, the hen pleased me
Fed my hen under yonder tree
Hen went chimmy-chuck, chimmy chuck
Cat went fiddle-eye, fiddle-eye fee

Bought me a duck, the duck pleased me
Fed that duck under yonder tree
Duck went quack quack
Hen went chimmy-chuck, chimmy chuck
Cat went fiddle-eye, fiddle-eye fee

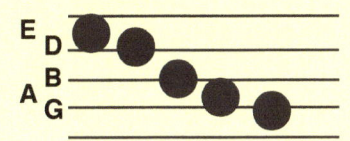

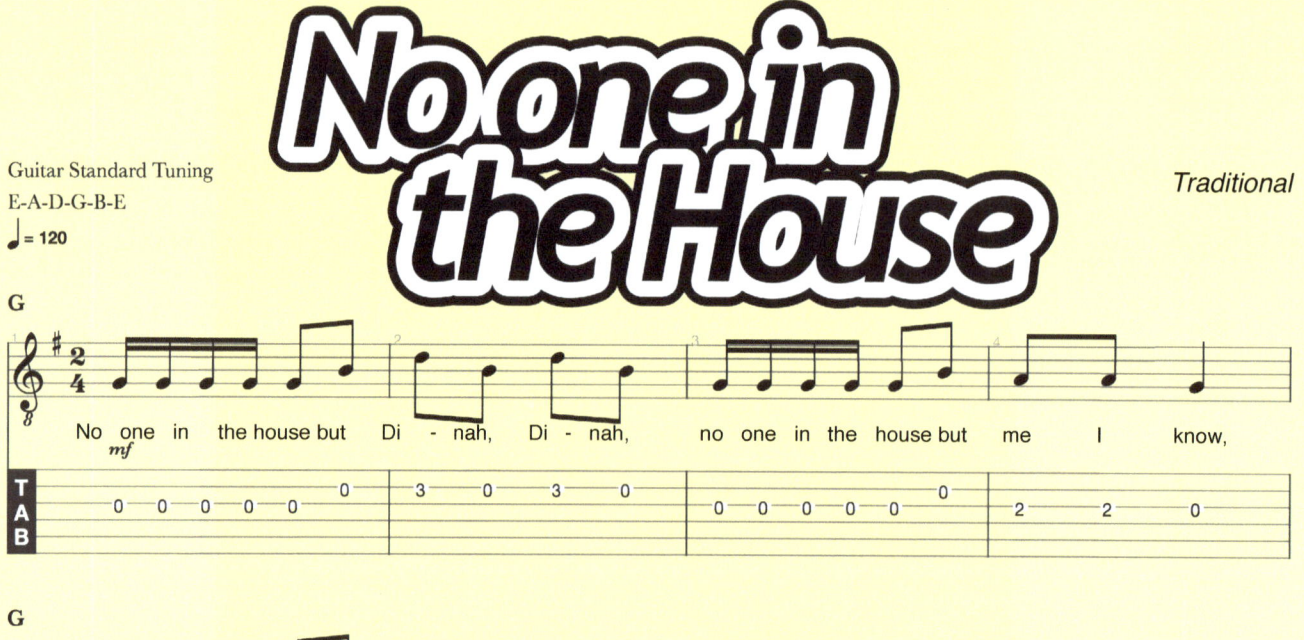

Guitar Standard Tuning
E-A-D-G-B-E
♩ = 120

Traditional

Down the Road

Guitar Standard Tuning
E-A-D-G-B-E
♩ = 120

Traditional

Down the road and a- cross the creek, can't get a let-ter but once a week,

I - da Red, I - da Blue, I got stuck on I - da too!

Next verses:

Down the road and across the creek
Can't get a letter but once a week
Ida Red, Ida Yellow
She has got another fellow

Down the road and across the creek
Can't get a letter but once a week
Ida Red, Ida Green
Prettiest girl I've ever seen

Down the road and across the creek
Can't get a letter but once a week
Ida Red, Ida Brown
Prettiest girl that rode into town

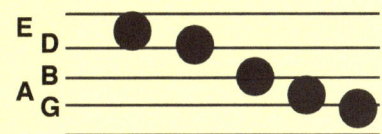

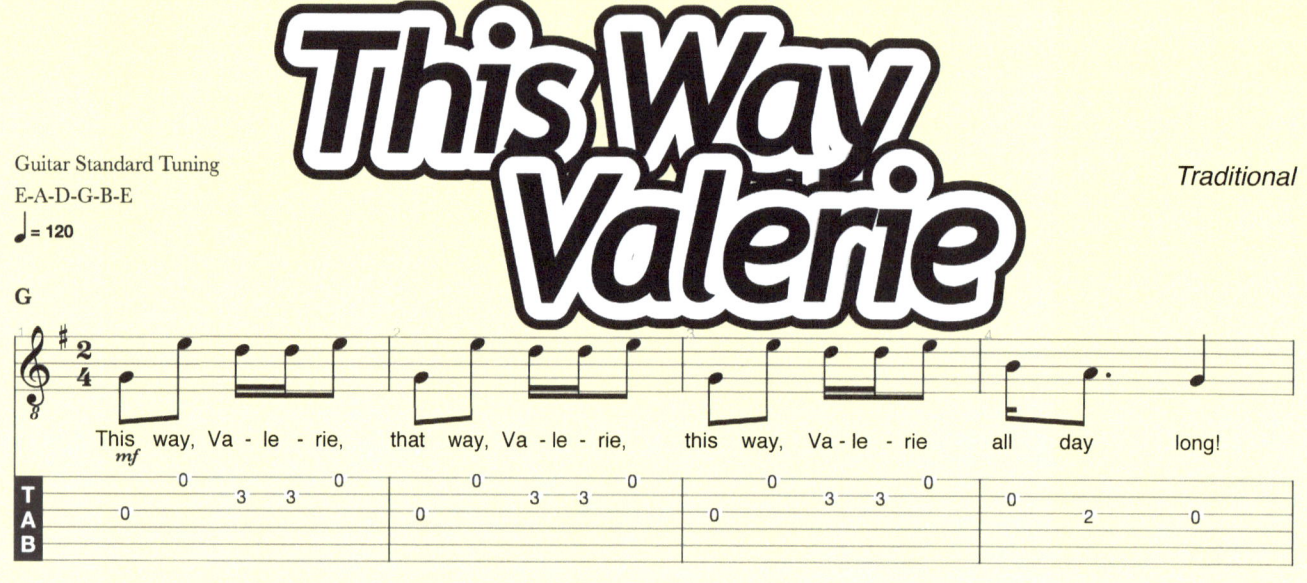

These pages introduce songs with 5 notes, and the different lengths of beats used:

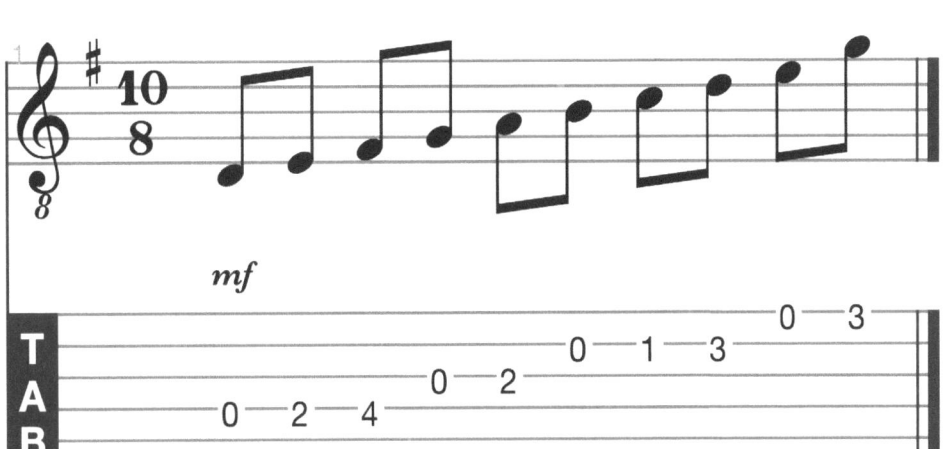

E is on the 1st open string
D is on the 2nd string, 3rd fret
C is on the 2nd string, 1st fret
B is on the 2nd open string
A is on the 3rd string, 2nd fret
G is on the 3rd open string
F# is on the 4th string, 4th fret
E is on the 4th string, 2nd fret
D is on the 4th open string

1st string
2nd string
3rd string
4th string
5th string
6th string

Semibreve/Whole Note
VERY SLOW WALK
(4 beats)

Minim/Half Note
SLOW WALK
(2 beats)

Crotchet/Quarter Note
WALK
(1 beat)

Quaver/Eighth Note
JOGGING
(half of a beat)

Semiquaver/Sixteenth Note
JOGGING QUICKLY
(quarter of a beat)

*Dotted quaver-semiquaver /
Dotted eighth note sixteenth note*
SKIPPING
(short-long)

*Semiquaver-dotted quaver /
Sixteenth note dotted eighth note*
GALLOP
(long-short)

*Quaver semiquaver /
Eighth note-sixteenth note*
"HAMBURGER"
(slow-quick-quick)

*Semiquaver-quaver /
Sixteenth note-eighth note*
"SAUSAGES"
(quick-quick slow)

Repeat the part between these signs

Little Bells

Guitar Standard Tuning
E-A-D-G-B-E
♩= 120

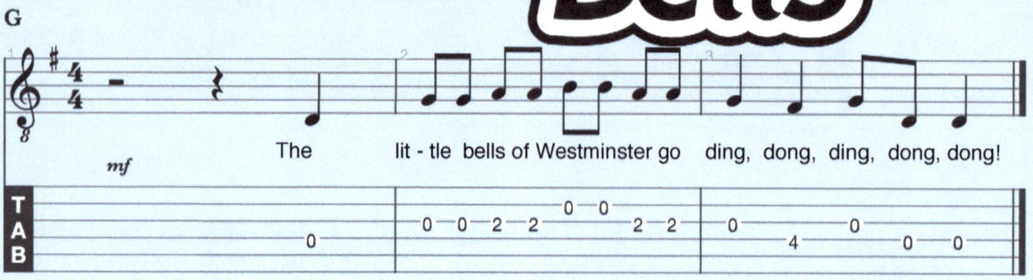

Traditional

G
mf
The lit - tle bells of Westminster go ding, dong, ding, dong, dong!
TAB
0
0 0 2 2 0 0 2 2
0 4 0 0 0

Watch Out!

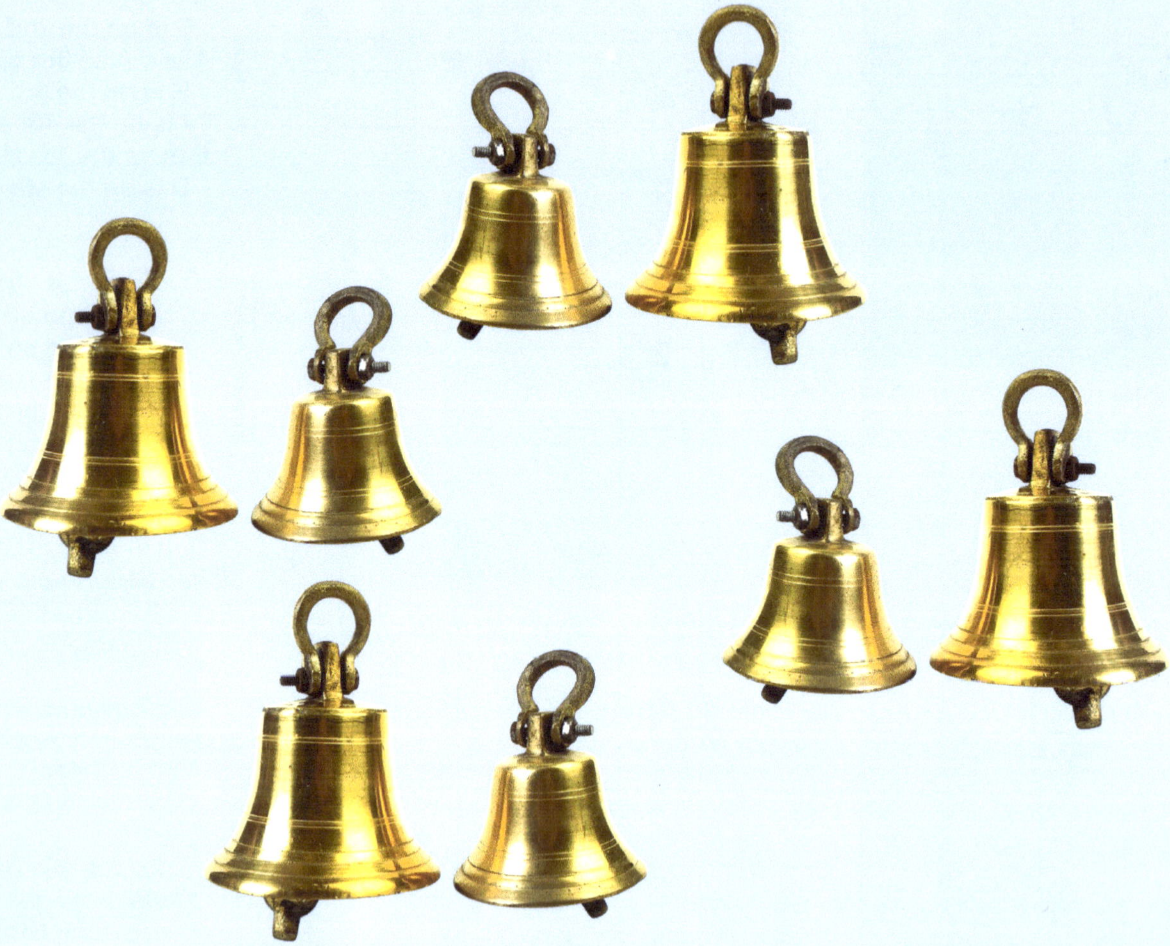

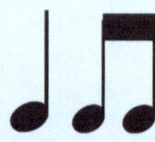

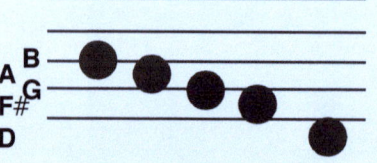

B
A
G
F#
D

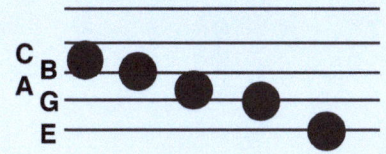

Circle to the Left

Traditional

Guitar Standard Tuning
E-A-D-G-B-E
♩ = 100

Cir-cle to the left, old brass wa-gon, cir-cle to the left, old brass wa-gon,

Cir-cle to the left, old brass wa-gon, you're the one my dar - ling!

Next verses:

Circle to the right, old brass wagon
Circle to the right, old brass wagon
Circle to the right, old brass wagon
You're the one my darling

Everybody down, old brass wagon
Everybody up, old brass wagon
Everybody down, old brass wagon
You're the one my darling

Everybody in, old brass wagon
Everybody out, old brass wagon
Everybody in, old brass wagon
You're the one my darling

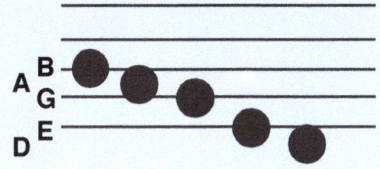

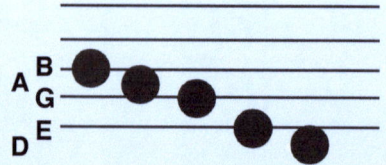

Guitar Standard Tuning
E-A-D-G-B-E
♩ = 120

Traditional

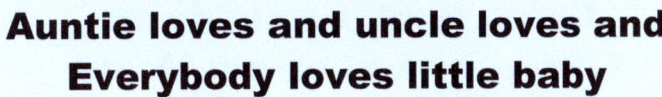

Mum - my loves and dad - dy loves and every - bo - dy loves lit - tle ba - by

Next verses:

Brother loves and sister loves and
Everybody loves little baby

Auntie loves and uncle loves and
Everybody loves little baby

Nanna loves and grandad loves and
Everybody loves little baby

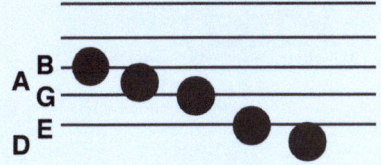

Circle Right

Guitar Standard Tuning
E-A-D-G-B-E
♩ = 120

Traditional

Cir-cle right, do-oh, do-oh, cir-cle right, do-oh, do-oh, cir-cle right, do-oh, do-oh, shake them simmons down!

Next verses:

Circle right, do-oh, do-oh
Circle right, do-oh, do-oh
Circle right, do-oh, do-oh
Shake them simmons down

Do-se-do, do-oh, do-oh
Do-se-do, do-oh, do-oh
Do-se-do, do-oh, do-oh
Shake them simmons down

Swing your partner, do-oh, do-oh
Swing your partner, do-oh, do-oh
Swing your partner, do-oh, do-oh
Shake them simmons down

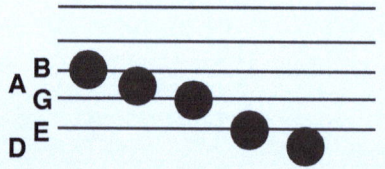

78

Oranges and Lemons

Guitar Standard Tuning
E-A-D-G-B-E
♩ = 110

Traditional

Oranges and le-mons, say the bells of Saint Cle-mens, you owe me two far-thing say the bells of Saint Mar-tins!

Next verse:

When will you pay me?
Say the bells of Old Bailey
When I grown rich
Say the bells of Shoreditch
When will that be?
Say the bells of Stepney
I do not know
Says the great bell of Bow

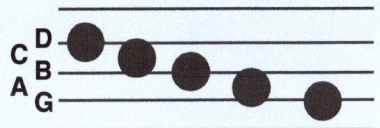

Skip to my Lou

Guitar Standard Tuning
E-A-D-G-B-E
♩= 120

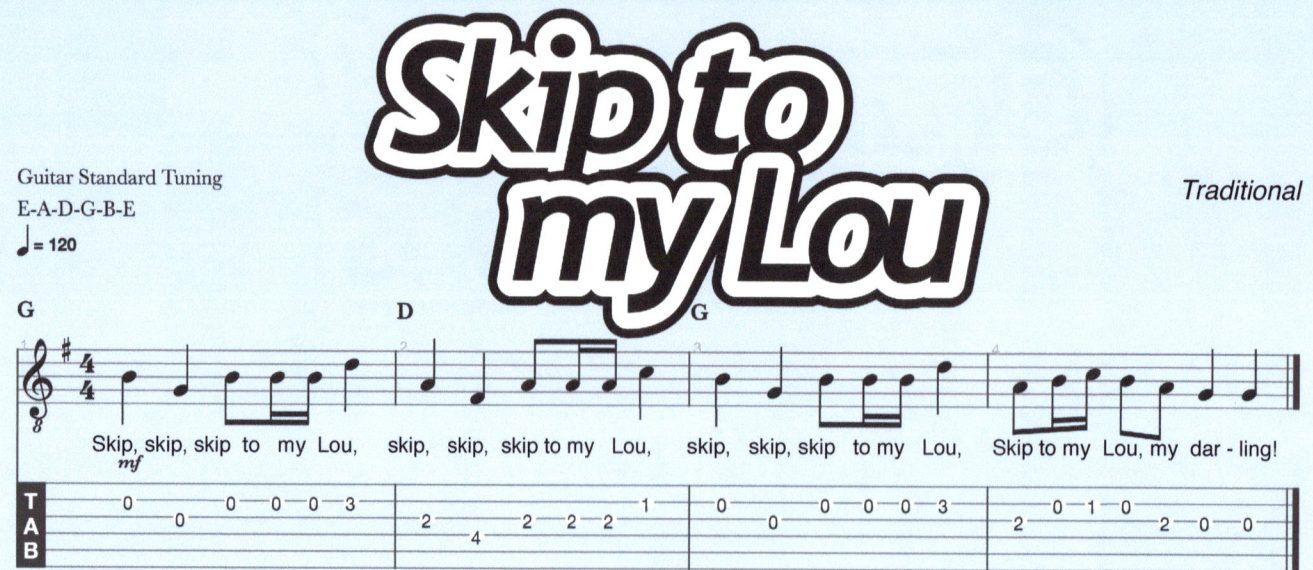

Traditional

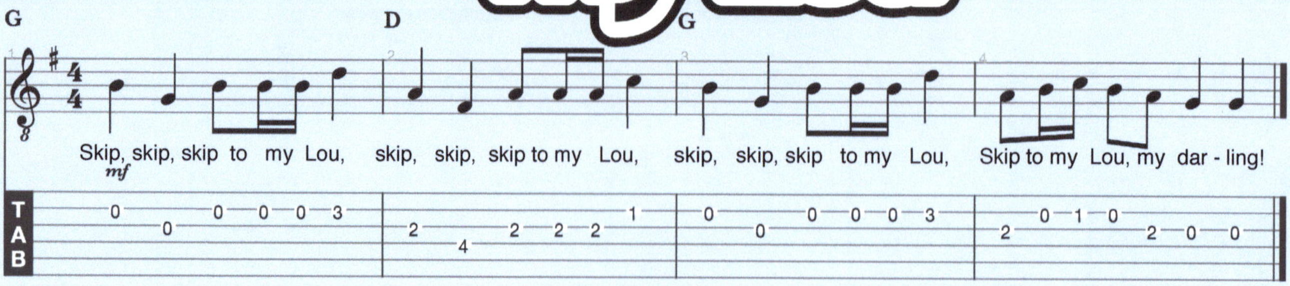
G
D
G
Skip, skip, skip to my Lou, skip, skip, skip to my Lou, skip, skip, skip to my Lou, Skip to my Lou, my dar - ling!
mf
TAB

Next verse:

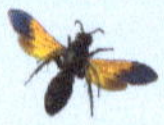

Fly in the buttermilk, shoo fly shoo
Fly in the buttermilk, shoo fly shoo
Fly in the buttermilk, shoo fly shoo
Skip to my Lou, my darling

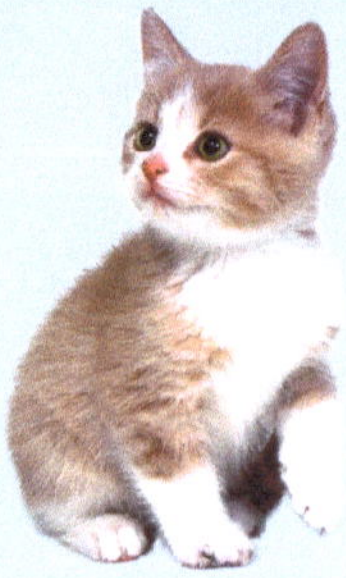

Cat's in the cream jar, what'll I do
Cat's in the cream jar, what'll I do
Cat's in the cream jar, what'll I do
Skip to my Lou, my darling

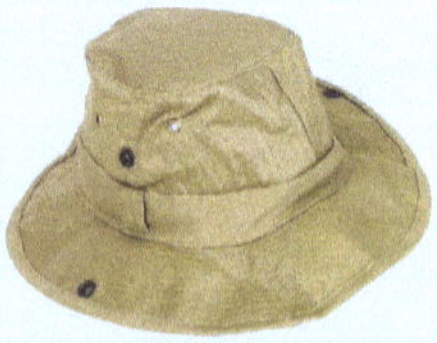

Dad's old hat got torn in two
Dad's old hat got torn in two
Dad's old hat got torn in two
Skip to my Lou, my darling

Watch Out!

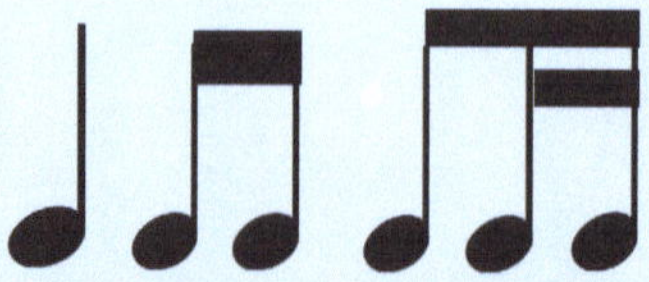

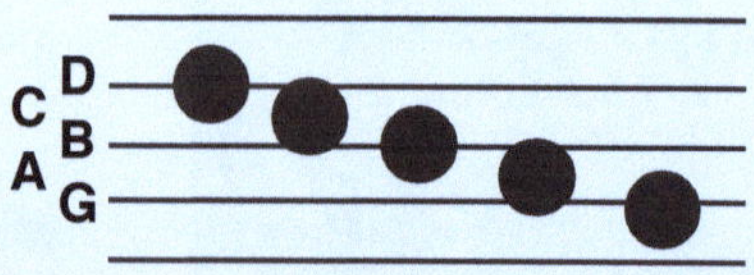
D
C
B
A
G

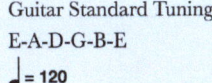

Traditional

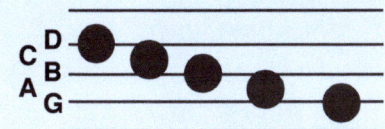

Orange Songs

These pages introduce songs with 6 to 9 notes, and the different lengths of beats used:

E is on the 1st open string
D is on the 2nd string, 3rd fret
C is on the 2nd string, 1st fret
B is on the 2nd open string
A is on the 3rd string, 2nd fret
G is on the 3rd open string
F# is on the 4th string, 4th fret
E is on the 4th string, 2nd fret
D is on the 4th open string

1st string
2nd string
3rd string
4th string
5th string
6th string

Semibreve/Whole Note
VERY SLOW WALK
(4 beats)

Minim/Half Note
SLOW WALK
(2 beats)

Crotchet/Quarter Note
WALK
(1 beat)

Quaver/Eighth Note
JOGGING
(half of a beat)

Semiquaver/Sixteenth Note
JOGGING QUICKLY
(quarter of a beat)

Dotted quaver-semiquaver / Dotted eighth note sixteenth note
SKIPPING
(short-long)

Semiquaver-dotted quaver / Sixteenth note dotted eighth note
GALLOP
(long-short)

Quaver semiquaver / Eighth note-sixteenth note
"HAMBURGER"
(slow-quick-quick)

Semiquaver-quaver / Sixteenth note-eighth note
"SAUSAGES"
(quick-quick slow)

Repeat the part between these signs

82

My Paddle

Guitar Standard Tuning
E-A-D-G-B-E
♩ = 120

Traditional

My pad - dle's keen and bright, fla - shing like sil - ver, fol - low the wild goose flight, dip - dip and swing,

Dip - dip and swing, dip dip, and swing!

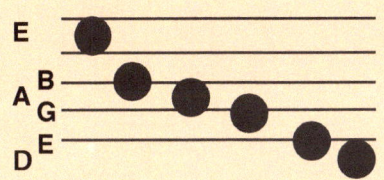

Over in the Meadow

Traditional

Guitar Standard Tuning
E-A-D-G-B-E
♩ = 120

O-ver in the meadow in the sand, in the sun, lived an old, mo-ther ti-ger and her lit-tle ti-ger one, "ROAR" said the mo-ther, "I ROAR!" said the one, so they roared and they roar-ed in the sa-nd, in the sun!

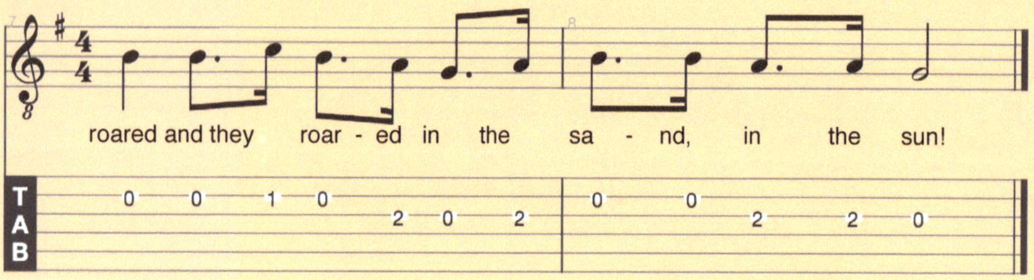

Next verse:

Over in the meadow where the stream runs so blue
Was an old mother elephant and her little calves two
"Stomp," said the mother, "we stomp," said the two
So they stomped and they stomped where the stream runs so blue

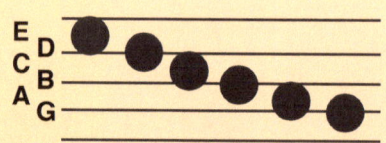

Guitar Standard Tuning
E-A-D-G-B-E
♩ = 120

Traditional

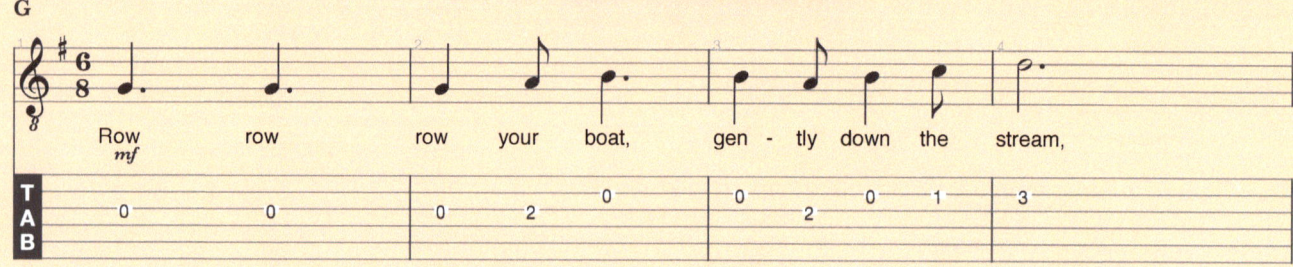

Next verse:

Row, row, row your boat
Gently down the stream
If you see a crocodile
Don't forget to scream

Row, row, row your boat
Gently to the shore
If you see a lion
Don't forget to ROAR!

Guitar Standard Tuning
E-A-D-G-B-E
♩ = 120

Traditional

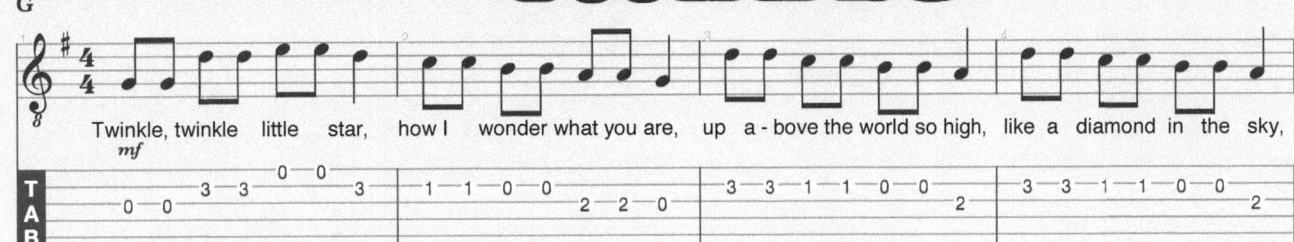

Twinkle, twinkle little star, how I wonder what you are, up a-bove the world so high, like a diamond in the sky,

Twinkle, twinkle little star, how I wonder what you are!

Next verse:

When the blazing sun has gone
When he nothing shines upon
Then you show your little light
Twinkle, twinkle through the night
Twinkle, twinkle little star
How I wonder what you are

In the dark blue sky so deep
Through my curtains often peep
For you never close your eyes
Til the morning sun does rise
Twinkle, twinkle little star
How I wonder what you are

London Bridge

Traditional

Guitar Standard Tuning
E-A-D-G-B-E
♩ = 120

London bridge is falling down, falling down, falling down, London bridge is falling down, my fair la - dy!

Next verse:

Build it up with wood and clay
Wood and clay, wood and clay
Build it up with wood and clay, my fair lady

Wood and clay will wash away
Wash away, wash away
Wood and clay will wash away, my fair lady

Build it up with bricks and mortar
Bricks and mortar, bricks and mortar
Build it up with bricks and mortar, my fair lady

Build it up with iron and steel
Iron and steel, iron and steel
Build it up with iron and steel, my fair lady

Build it up with silver and gold
Silver and gold, silver and gold
Build it up with silver and gold, my fair lady

  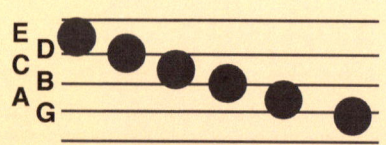

This old Man

Traditional

Guitar Standard Tuning
E-A-D-G-B-E
♩ = 120

This old man, he played one, he played nic-nac on my drum with a nic-nac, paddy whack, give a dog a bone, this old man came rolling home!

Next verse:

This old man, he played two, he played nicnac on my shoe
With a nicnac paddy whack, give a dog a bone
This old man came rolling home

This old man, he played three, he played nicnac on my knee
With a nicnac paddy whack, give a dog a bone
This old man came rolling home

This old man, he played four, he played nicnac on my door
With a nicnac paddy whack, give a dog a bone
This old man came rolling home

This old man, he played five, he played nicnac on my hive
With a nicnac paddy whack, give a dog a bone
This old man came rolling home

This old man, he played six, he played nicnac on my sticks
With a nicnac paddy whack, give a dog a bone
This old man came rolling home

Watch Out!

Ring a Rosies

Guitar Standard Tuning
E-A-D-G-B-E
♩ = 120

Traditional

G

Ring a ring a ro-sies a pocket full of po-sies a-ti-shoo a-ti-shoo, we all fall down!

Watch Out!

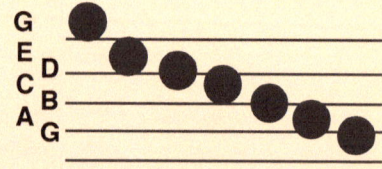

Traditional

Guitar Standard Tuning
E-A-D-G-B-E
♩ = 120

Love some-bo-dy, yes, I do, love some-bo-dy, yes, I do,

Love some-bo-dy, yes, I do, love some-bo-dy, and it's you, you, you!

Next verse:

Love somebody
Yes I do
Love somebody
Yes I do
Love somebody
Yes I do
Love somebody
But I won't say who!

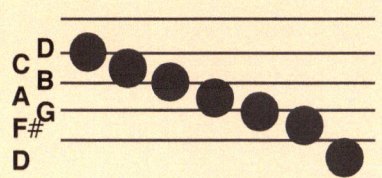

Traditional

Guitar Standard Tuning
E-A-D-G-B-E
♩ = 200

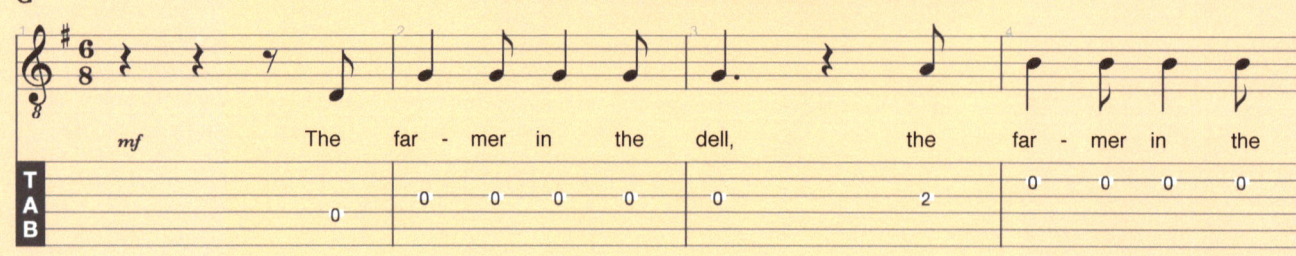

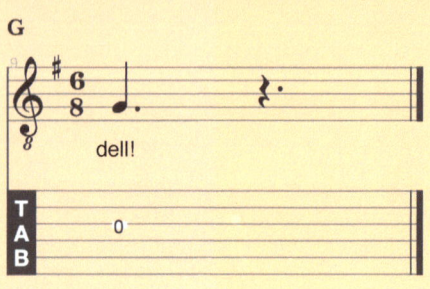

Next verse:

The farmer has a wife, the farmer has a wife, E-I-N-D-O ...
The wife has a child, the wife has a child, E-I-N-D-O ...
The child has a dog, the child has a dog, E-I-N-D-O ...
The dog has a cat, the dog has a cat, E-I-N-D-O ...
The cat has a mouse, the cat has a mouse, E-I-N-D-O ...
The mouse has a cheese, the mouse has a cheese, E-I-N-D-O ...
We all pat the cheese, we all pat the cheese, E-I-N-D-O ...

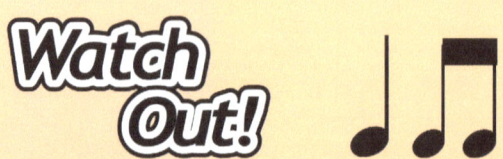
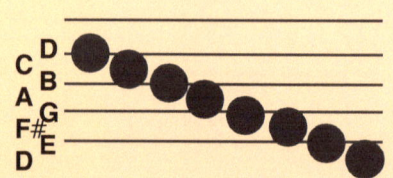

Darling Clementine

Traditional

Guitar Standard Tuning
E-A-D-G-B-E
♩ = 120

in a ca - vern, in a can - yon, ex - ca - va - ting for a

mine, lived a mi - ner, for - ty ni - ner, and his daugh - ter, Cle - men

tine!

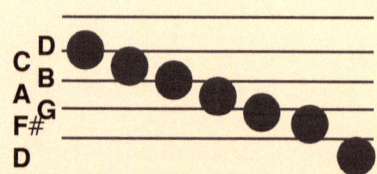

My Bonnie

Traditional

Guitar Standard Tuning
E-A-D-G-B-E
♩ = 120

My Bonnie lies o-ver the o-cean, my Bonnie lies o-ver the sea, My Bonnie lies o-ver the o-cean, oh, bring back my Bon-nie to me, Bring back, oh, bring back, oh, bring back my Bon-nie to me, to me, Bring back, oh, bring back, oh, bring back my Bon-nie to me!

Oh blow you waves over the ocean
Oh blow you waves over the sea
Oh blow you waves over the ocean
And bring back my Bonnie to me

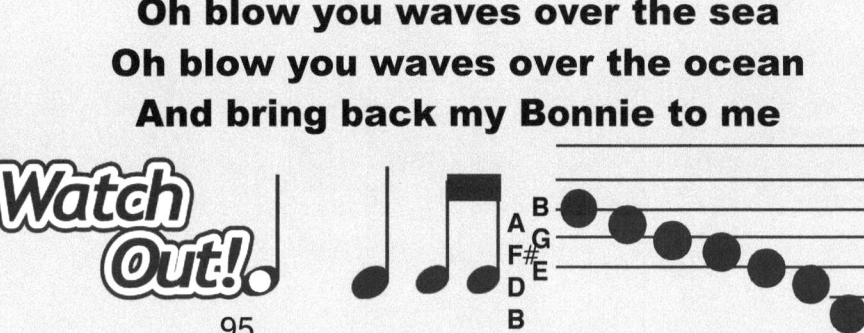

Muffin Man

Traditional

Guitar Standard Tuning
E-A-D-G-B-E
♩ = 120

Next verse:

Yes I know the muffin man
The muffin man, the muffin man
Yes I know the muffin man
Who lives on Drury Lane

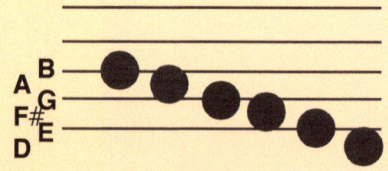

Guitar Standard Tuning
E-A-D-G-B-E

♩ = 200

Traditional

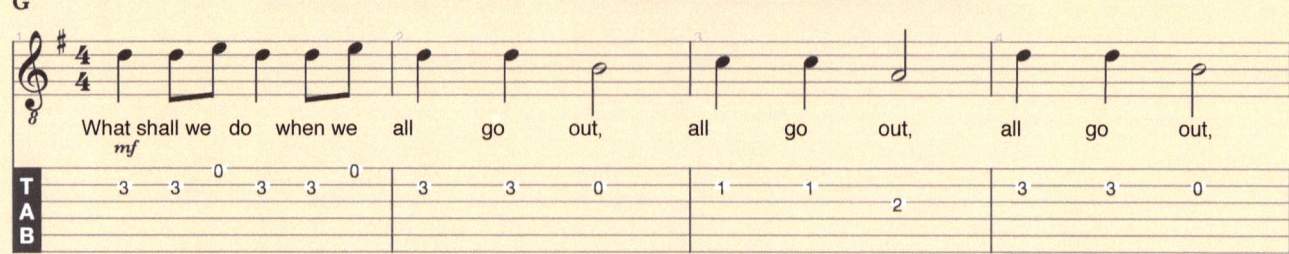

What shall we do when we all go out, all go out, all go out,

What shall we do when we all go out, when we all go out to play!

Next verse:

Let's all play on the merry-go-round
The merry-go-round, the merry-go-round
Let's all play on the merry-go-round
When we all go out to play

Let's all play on the see saw
The see saw, the see saw
Let's all play on the see saw
When we all go out to play

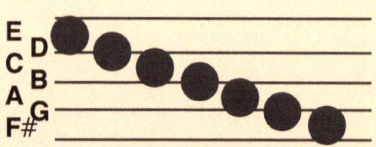

Guitar Standard Tuning
E-A-D-G-B-E
♩ = 120

Traditional

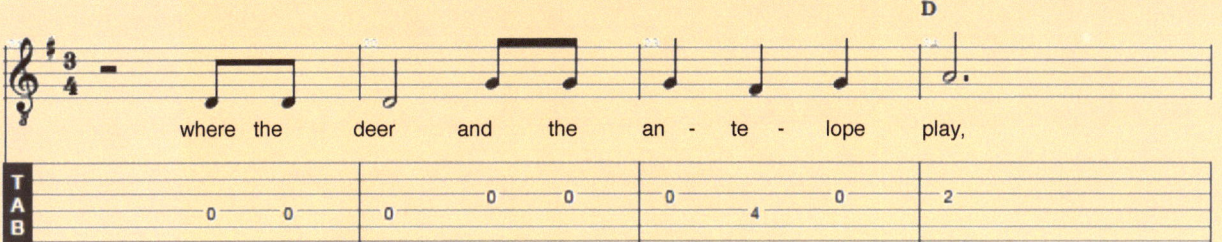

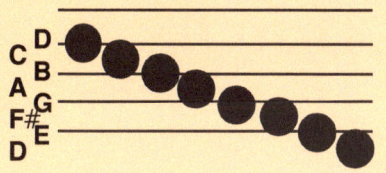

Polly put the Kettle on

Guitar Standard Tuning
E-A-D-G-B-E
♩ = 120

Traditional

Pol-ly put the ket-tle on, Pol-ly put the ket-tle on, Pol-ly put the ket-tle on, we'll all have tea!

Next verse:

Sukey take it off again
Sukey take it off again
Sukey take it off again
They've all gone away

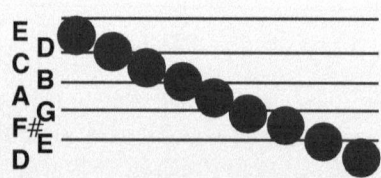

102

Drunken Sailor

Guitar Standard Tuning
E-A-D-G-B-E
♩ = 200

Traditional

What shall we do with a drun-ken sai-lor, what shall we do with a drun-ken sai-lor,

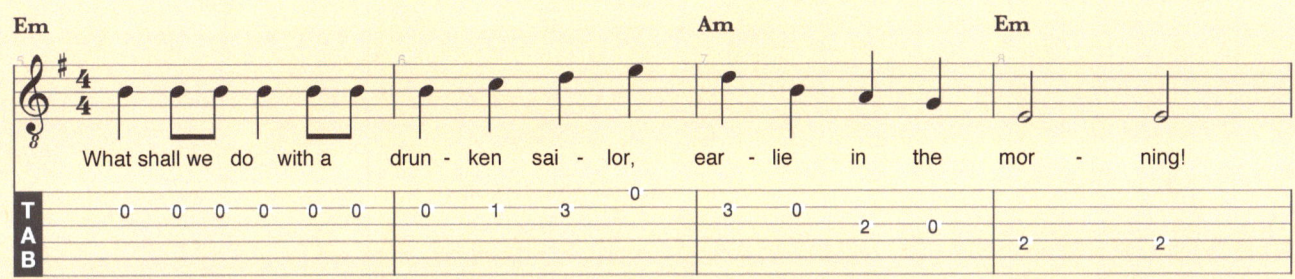

What shall we do with a drun-ken sai-lor, ear-lie in the mor-ning!

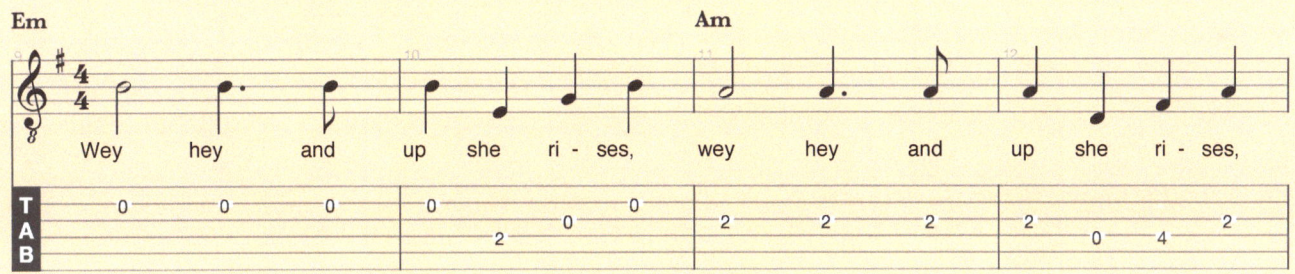

Wey hey and up she ri-ses, wey hey and up she ri-ses,

Wey hey and up she ri-ses, ear-lie in the mor-ning!

Make him work and make him bail her
Make him work and make him bail her
Make him work and make him bail her
Earlie in the morning

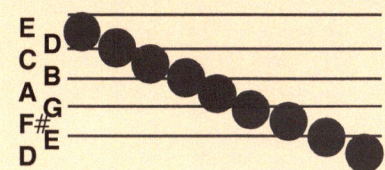

Index of Songs

Aiken Drum	93
A Tisket A Tasket	24
Andy Pandy	31
Apple Tree	34
Around the Buttercup	56
Bell Horses	25
Bobby Shaftoe	21
Bought me a Cat	63
Bounce High	18
Bow Wow Wow	54
Built My Lady	67
Charlie over the Ocean	46
Chase the Squirrel	35
Circle to the Left	75
Circle Right	78
Cobbler Cobbler	10
Come Butter	45
Coming Round the Mountain	97
Darling Clementine	94
Doggie Doggie	16
Do Pity My Case	68
Down the Road	69
Drunken Sailor	103
Farmer in the Dell	92
Frosty Weather	53
G-Scale	104
Go Round the Mountain	43
Hey Jim-along	48
Here Comes a Bluebird	60
Hickory Dickory	29
Home on the Range	100
Hop Old Squirrel	39
Hot Cross Buns	38
How Many Miles	65
Hush Little Baby	50
Ickle Ockle	36
I had a Dog	22
I have Lost	37
John Kinaker	57
Johnny Works	61
Lemonade	26
Little Bells	72
Lil Liza Jane	85
London Bridge	88
Love Somebody	91

Lucy Locket	15
Mary had a Little Lamb	40
Muffin Man	96
Mummy Loves	77
My Bonnie	95
My Paddle	83
No one in the House	64
Oats and Beans	51
Old King Glory	76
Old Mister Rabbit	47
On a Log	33
Once a Man	52
Oranges and Lemons	79
Over in the Meadow	84
Pease Porridge	30
Phoebe, Phoebe	73
Polly Put the Kettle On	102
Poor Little Kitty Cat	44
Pretty Little Susie	99
Pumpkin Pumpkin	66
Rabbit Run	81
Rain Rain	11
Red Rover	20
Riding in a Buggy	41
Ring a Rosies	90
Rosie Darling	42
Round and Round	14
Row Row Row	86
Sally Go Round the Sun	55
See Saw	13
See Saw Margery Daw	23
Skip to my Lou	80
Snail Snail	17
Starlight	12
Teddy Bear	32
There was a jolly miller	74
This Old Man	89
This Way Valerie	70
Tideo	58
Twinkle Twinkle	87
We are Dancing	19
What Shall We Do	98
Where are you Going?	27
Who Did All the Baking	59
Who's That?	62

ABOUT THE AUTHOR

Frances has presented early years music sessions in a variety of settings since 2006, after training as a secondary mathematics and science teacher. She is fascinated by research into the health, educational and developmental benefits of music. Not content with being involved with children's music alone, she directs a local community choir, the Warblers.

www.ingramcontent.com/pod-product-compliance
Lightning Source LLC
Chambersburg PA
CBHW041525220426
43670CB00002B/36